O. DUNCAN. 97

The Roots of

Healing

are in the

Earth

The Roots of

Healing

are in the

Earth

A Journey into Medical Anthropology

William Evans, M.D.

An Integration of Teachings from
        Tu Moonwalker
        Lané Saán
        Jonas Salk
        Albert Schweitzer

For information address
        Clearwater Pools Publishing
        P. O. Box 242
        Carbondale, Colorado 81623

Library of Congress Catalog
Number 97-091849

ISBN   0-9619258-3-1 Hard Cover
            0-9619258-4-1 Soft Cover

Acknowledgments

The creation of this book would not have happened without the inspiration, teaching, and wisdom of many people. I thank those mentors who believed in me and passed their gifts. I stand on their shoulders. My friend Jesse Lilienthal inspired me to always remain a student. This book is an integration of what four important teachers have shared with me from their understanding of life. At the nucleus is Tu Moonwalker. When I first met Tu in 1991 and talked with her of my desire to "write about health and medicine," my hesitations were holding me back. She looked at me and said, "I think you ought to do it."

That blessing made all of the difference in the world, for the written words began to flow. Later Tu suggested this book. Without her faithful support this work would not have come to be. Many hours of conversation and teaching with her refined the concepts which follow. The source of the teaching and understanding about the 'right to be,' which has grown strong in me, is from Tu and her able and vigorous ceremonial leader Lané Saán. Without their guidance my understanding of what Jonas Salk and Albert Schweitzer taught would not yet have come active in my life and work.

When Jonas Salk spoke to me in 1975 of Schools of Health, I said to him, "That is what I am to do; where do I go?" Salk said, "There isn't any place." But these two native women, Lané and Tu, were able to help me understand what Salk and Schweitzer knew. My purpose is to energize the seed of this collective vision so that the meaning of health might come alive in our children and culture. This will happen only when we know the roots of health in the earth and ourselves.

Clifford Duncan's pen-and-ink drawings reveal the eye and hand guided by the beauty of his Ute spirit, moving with the rhythm of the earth.

Giles Florence for editing the manuscript, Ken Johnson for his able and generous guidance in printing and Chan Edmonds for page layout.

Cover color separation and rainbow by Gran Farnum Printing.

I thank all of those who have walked and talked with me, sharing their wisdom: Gretchen Bering, Page Bailey, Bob Brittain, Bill Campbell, Tom Carey, Marc Choyt, Kara Evans, Lucy Evans, Margaret Evans, Marian Evans, Sarah Evans, Thos Evans, Bob Goldhammer, Bertha Gotterup, Patricia Hopkins, Bill Kight, Cindy Knudson, Gale Litvak, Dick and Rita Marsh, Christina MacLeod, Bill McClure, Kathleen Menten, Roderick O'Conner, Valerie Pacini, Julie Paxton, Bernadette Prinster, Edgel Pyles, Jonathan Showstack, Edie Swan, Henry Swan, April Szabo, George Tolles, Tim Windle, and Trudy Welty.

For the health
of my children
and their children
for seven generations to come.

The Teachers

Tu Moonwalker was born into an Apache family of the medicine way. She began her studies before puberty under the tutelage of her grandmother. She has learned to heal and live through intimate experience with the earth, plants and animals. She is a guardian of the earth.

Lané Saán comes from Jewish and Yaqui parentage. Her healing and spiritual training began from these two traditions. Her life work is one of respect for the earth and tradition of wisdom. She is an ordained minister and teacher.

Jonas Salk was born in New York City, the oldest son of a garment industry worker. He helped pay for his education by working after school and earning scholarships. He graduated from the New York University School of Medicine in 1939. He developed the first effective vaccine against poliomyelitis. In 1964 he became the director of the Salk Institute for Biological Sciences in La Jolla, California. In 1973 he published the *The Survival of the Wisest,* a hypothesis that wisdom is of practical value for human survival and for the enhancement of the quality of life. Salk proposed that humans can learn wisdom from nature.

Albert Schweitzer was a philosopher, physician, musician, clergyman, missionary and writer. He was born in 1875 near Strasbourg in Upper Alsace. The second child of a Protestant minister, he was a mythic figure of this century, not without controversy. His only visit to the United States was to Aspen, Colorado. Schweitzer espoused reverence for life, world peace, and warned against the dangers of conflict, atomic weapons, and war. He received the Nobel Peace Prize in 1952.

The root idea of my theory of the universe is that my relation to my own being and to the objective world is determined by reverence for life.

Albert Schweitzer

You have a right to be a part of the whole.

Tu Moonwalker

CONTENTS

INTRODUCTION

Ben Franklin was an astute observer. Not much slipped past Ben unnoticed. As the official printer for the colony of Pennsylvania he became acquainted with Indian political organizations. Many people do not realize how significant this was to the young colonies. Ben published the records and speeches of the various Indian assemblies and treaty negotiations. His instinctive curiosity led him into a study of Indian culture and institutions. Because of his expertise in Indian matters the colonial government of Pennsylvania offered him his first diplomatic appointment as their Indian commissioner. While in this capacity in the 1750s he became intimately familiar with the intricacies of Indian political culture and especially the League of the Iroquois.

Well done is better than well said.

- Ben Franklin

The League of the Iroquois was founded sometime between 1000 and 1450 AD under a constitution called the Great Law of Peace. The first person to propose a union of the original thirteen colonies was Canassatego, an Iroquois chief who spoke at an Indian-British assembly in 1744 in Pennsylvania. He complained that the Indians found it difficult to deal with the different colonial administrations, each with its own policy. He suggested life would be easier for everyone if the colonists could have a union which allowed them to speak with one voice and suggested that they do as his people had done and form a union like the League of the Iroquois.

The thirteen original colonies were populated by a strong-willed independent stock of people who fled Europe for the new world. Although they gathered under the Articles of Confederation they were thirteen separate and sovereign states. How could one country be forged out of all thirteen without each one yielding its own power?[1] American democracy owes its distinctive character to the principles and structure of American Indian civil government.[2]

Following his experience in Indian diplomacy, Ben Franklin became a lifelong champion of the Indian political structure and advocated its use by the Americans. He proposed that the new American government incorporate many of the same features as the government of the Iroquois. At the 1754 Albany Congress, Franklin called on the colonies to unite and emulate the Iroquois League; this call was not heeded until the Constitution was written three decades later. Charles Thomson, the perpetual secretary of the Continental Congress, was also a student of the Iroquois political organization. The Delaware Nation adopted him as a full member because he spent so much energy studying the Indians and their way of life.

Wish not so much to live long, as to live well.

- Ben Franklin

The Founding Fathers were faced with a major problem when it came time to invent the government of the United States, and they found the inspiration for the new America in the Great Law of Peace of the League of Iroquois.[3] This concept was later extended in 1918 with the establishment of the League of Nations and more recently underlay creation of the General Assembly of the United Nations.[4] This gift is one of many that have come from the native people of the new world. Also among these gifts are medical and health concepts which have been widely accepted.

One such example is the vitamin-C that was contained in the juice and sap of a certain tree the local Indian chief, Domagaia, prescribed for Jacques Cartier and his men as they were dying of scurvy in the bitter cold winter of 1535-36.

Twenty-five men of the expedition died before Cartier found Domagaia. All of those treated recovered, and the Frenchmen marveled at the curative skill of the natives.[5]

This book describes another gift that is a central concept of Native American philosophy that has not been widely understood and claimed. Like Vitamin C it has significant health implications. It is, in fact, my suggestion that this concept is fundamental to a coherent view of health and self responsibility. While I do not advocate that we try to become Native Americans, I suggest that we learn from them. Just as we looked at their form of democracy and developed our own version, I propose a careful look at their concept of self perception. This concept is fundamental to personal accountability and healthy function. Chapter 4 describes existing communication and perceptual applications of this principle already functioning in activities and organizations within mainstream American society. Chapter 5 makes a distinction between medical care and health care, and advocates training in "educational therapeutics" for physicians. This bridging between medicine and health is illustrated with a discussion of low back pain.

And he said when you get rid of that anger and resentment toward whites for what they have done, everything you ask with His name (the Creator) will come to you—no difficulty. Because you have built a compassion inside of you to the human race of the world. See,

Life consists of what a man is thinking all of the day.

- Ralph Waldo Emerson

that is what they were talking about.
Eddie Box, Ute Elder and Medicine Man
American Indian[6]

Health is like the grass pushing up between the cracks in the sidewalk. It is an ever-present force, seeking expression. The rhythm of my heartbeat aligns with health or sickness. The first step on the journey toward health is to respect my self—trust who I am. Only if I trust myself can my journey become coherent. As Antonovsky notes, "We are coming to understand health not so much as the absence of disease, but rather the sense of coherence that makes life comprehensible, manageable, and meaningful in the presence of change in ourselves and the environment around us."[7] Knowing and trusting who I am is the foundation of my health. Claiming health begins with claiming one's 'right to be' a part of the whole. Eddie Box, Sr., models for us the level of health possible when that wholeness includes the healing spirit which enables one to overcome great anger, fear, or grief and loss.

Only an individual has a mind. Hence, only an individual can say how he or she sees the world.

- Aaron Antonovsky

Health can also be fragile and snap as quickly as a dry twig in winter. We can travel to health as swiftly and directly as an arrow in flight. Or the search can be a confusing struggle of trying to bring warring factions to cooperation. Some people quickly see a path through the layers of advice and criticism, and for others the way is obscured by doubt and fear. As we have become a technological culture the "ease and convenience" of our lifestyle distances us from nature, ourselves, and many of the fundamentals of health. When we stand on asphalt or concrete or when we dwell and work enclosed by steel and glass it is more difficult for the rhythm of our heartbeat to move with the rhythm of the earth.

Health is a cooperative process. My mind, body, emotions, heart, lungs, brain, hands, and essence have all cooperated for me to send these thoughts to you. My lungs didn't say, "This fellow has been thinking too much lately, I am going to take the morning off and go down to the pool at the hot springs. I am not going to take in any more oxygen for his brain." No, my breathing, the rhythm of my heart, and my thinking have all come to an agreement, to sit down and write these words. There is, of course, also a competitive dimension to health. Our white blood cells defend us against invaders and attack virulent bacteria and viruses. Health has both cooperative and competitive dimensions.

When we are seeking something, the modern approach seems to be one of analyzing the situation, pinpointing the problem, and finding a successful strategy and solution. Analysis leads us to separate components in order to find the strategy of choice. Indeed this can be very successful. Analysis has become the dominant strategy in medicine for finding the cause and treatment of specific diseases. But as we witness the fragmentation and polarization of families, communities, and ourselves we begin to see that on many occasions what is needed is not more analysis and competition, but cooperation, synthesis, and synergy. Such coming together, such bridging, can be healing because analytical methods tend to separate and disconnect. How do we call together the scattered interdependent parts that need to cooperate in order for the whole to function as a unit? What conditions favor synergy? Healing involves all our parts: mind, body, emotions, and essence. Essence is soul, the immortal core of our being. To heal means to make whole. Failure to actively claim our wholeness, our 'right to be,' is a refusal of the great gift bestowed upon us by our creator.

Sythesis is more important than analysis, context more important than specialization.

- Joachim-Ernst Berendt

*I think it takes
courage to realize
that we are whole.*

- Dhyani Ywahoo

The most ancient oral and written traditions available to us acknowledge the importance of the balance of and relationship between the physical, mental, emotional, and spiritual. St. Mark recorded the first of all commandments to be love for the Creator "with all thy heart, and with all thy soul, and with all thy mind, and with all thy strength."[8] But we may not find support for such integrated wholeness in our lives, when we are called to divide mind from body in order to get the job done, stuff our emotions while we do it and, for certain, "don't bring your soul in here to work". Internal fracture and fragmentation is fissuring through individuals, families, and the larger culture at an accelerating speed. Medical care is a powerful resource in the quest for health, but it has not mended these fractures.

The successes of the modern medical model are based on identifying what has gone wrong, analyzing the pathology, and treating the problem. Medicine is a competitive model. Physicians are trained to defeat disease and battle infection. As a doctor I want an antibiotic that will kill your infection. We applaud medical victories over pathology. A good example is what Jonas Salk did with polio. He understood the viral etiology of the disease and developed an effective vaccine to prevent poliomyelitis. For those fortunate enough to receive that vaccine in time, polio was defeated. Medically, physicians wage war against disease.

In fact, for most of our lives, many of us have lived in a war paradigm. War seemed to be the only solution to deal with Hitler and it was effective. We think in terms of war being the most effective strategy. We are engaged in wars on AIDS, cancer, street drugs, illiteracy, and poverty to name a few. But a language and strategy of war has limitations. It does not work well when we turn it on each other, our children, ourselves, or the earth.

A significant flaw entered our language and thinking a few years ago, when insurance companies changed the name of medical insurance to health insurance. They did this because the rising costs of medical care necessitated a reduction in benefits and an increase in policy deductibles. These shrewd corporations were faced with a marketing challenge: how to charge more for a product and sell less of it. They hit upon a bold stroke of genius, they decided to call medical insurance by a new name—health insurance. A more positive and robust product was projected, and it took. Politicians, doctors, and hospitals fell into line, adopted the new language and played the game. Now medical care is widely called health care. But this blurring of the distinction between medicine and health, implies that health will be achieved through a medical strategy to defeat the disease. The strategy assumes that if we analyze the need correctly and attack at the right place, we will find health. Wrong! Health is a cooperative process. Health in our time will not be achieved through a war paradigm; that is an illusion. Medical care is valuable, but it is only a tool to help us. Following the path of medicine will not take me to the whole of health.

But unless you are conscious that health is a cooperative process and involves more than medical care— you may not see the illusion the culture is following. The successes of medicine are wonderful, but there are also failures and disorders not responding to modern medical technology. For example, many conditions of chronic disability do not correlate with organic pathology but rather with job dissatisfaction. The

Since the early 1970s we have come to understand that science without wisdom can be dangerous.

- Joachim-Ernst Berendt

meaning of the work we do becomes physically active in our bodies. Anger-driven movement[9] can accumulate in the bodies of unhappy workers as painful dysfunction. Over 45 percent of Americans living at home have one or more chronic conditions, and their direct medical care costs now account for three quarters of US medical care expenditures.[10] Health is the result of many cooperative processes; we are participants in a dance of interdependence with all of creation. Jonas Salk saw this when he observed, "Until we see the sources of pathology as partly attributable to ignorance of what is required for maintaining health, we will continue to search for causes which can be eliminated or prevented, when, in fact, some of the pathology we seek to suppress is the result of our failure to do certain things that actively evoke and maintain a state of balance."[11] The distinction between medical care and health care was so clear for Salk that as early as 1975 he was advocating schools of health based on the art and science of balanced wellbeing in addition to schools of medicine based on diagnosing and treating pathology.

How do we find balance? Where do I look? Bertha Grove, a Ute Elder reminded me, "As you go, don't forget the harmony within you and around you that holds it all together." I can easily lose the harmony within me and become frightened. When that happens I need to create conditions that actively evoke and support my balance and recall that there is a power greater than my fear. When things get tough I need to walk up on the ridge and look at the valley, at the mountains all around and see that beauty in order to again feel the rhythm of the earth. On that higher ground I experience a larger perspective and spirit, the hurry and fear on the highways and in the towns below is a human choice and creation. Fear can be all

Man has reached a point, occuring in our time, when an epochal change is being experienced.

- Jonas Salk

consuming or it can be an emotion flowing through me that is a motivator—not my total being. Becoming dominated by an emotion, fear, for example, is one way in which I can fragment and lose contact with my other parts.

When I am scattered I don't trust my wholeness, but rather confuse my fear with my total being. I may grasp at material symbols. My bank account becomes my identity. Climbing up on the ridge restores the balance, the inner and outer harmonies. The relationships between my mind, body, emotions, and essence with the world. I am nourished by the enormous beauty of nature around me. A tree does not participate in the forest with only branches and leaves, it sends its roots deep into the soil. Like all of nature, the roots of my survival and my health are intertwined with the earth and the world around me.

To be healthy requires that I have the intention to be whole. A clear intention is a total commitment. I am not an isolated entity. I participate in a family, a community, a profession, a state, a nation, and the world. A world which is part of all creation. The measure of my participation and presence is whether my being and doing is meaningful. If I align my gifts and talents with meaningful purpose and the contribution is affirmed, I am blessed. My life is growing in fertile soil. If I am rejected, shunned or shamed by my family, profession, or community I shrivel. My purpose needs community. Meaningful purpose and relationships may have more to do with my health than with medical care.

What can be done to evoke and support a healthy and meaningful harmony between the internal and external? Words are powerful medicine. They flow from the

Learn to say no; it will be of more use to you than being able to read Latin.

- Charles Haddon Spurgeon

*Climb the mountains
and get their good
tidings;
nature's peace will flow
into you as
sunshine into flowers;
the winds will
blow their freshness
into you and the
storms their energy,
and cares will
drop off like
autumn leaves.*

- John Muir

core of our being. The very manner of how I speak to others or am spoken to can have a healing or wounding quality. How I see and am seen will either call forth my talents or shut me down. How I relate to others connects me with all generations and the whole of human beings or isolates me in loneliness. The heart of healing is inclusive not exclusive. The ego is easily frightened and when it feels threatened it will attack. That can be fearful and can eventually become pathologic. The only agreement that can hold it all together is the agreement to seek that which is best for all concerned, including oneself. In that field of vision medical care can be seen to cooperate in playing a meaningful part in creating the whole of health.

In order to claim the harmony within me and around me that holds it all together I must know who I am. That requires the knowing to be accompanied by an integration of my body, mind, emotions, and essence. The spirit of health is unique to each individual. Medical care applies scientific principles to large numbers of people and directs attention to useful generalizations and treatment plans. But you are one of a kind—one who may also have specific health needs, which you must learn to identify and trust.

This may sound vague and non-specific to those seeking only hard objective information, but the human soul is very real and it is our connection to all creation. In 1949 at Aspen, Colorado, Hutchins and Borgese prepared a statement for the Goethe Bicentennial Festival that included this observation:

The difficulty of our time is a difficulty of the human spirit. We have to abandon the illusion, which some of our ancestors were able to cherish, that our difficulty is primarily political, economic, technological, or edu-

cational. The social order has been rearranged, and old evils appear under new names. Literacy has flourished, and taste has been debased. Goods have been produced and distributed in untold quantities and blown up in untold quantities. Things seem to be bigger; they do not seem to be better. We are at last face to face with the fact that our difficulty is a difficulty of the human spirit.[12]

Disciplining the mind to reclaim the soul requires accessing and respecting those subtle and invisible feelings and qualities at the roots of our being. The only time Albert Schweitzer came to America was for the Goethe Festival in Aspen. He said, "The root-idea of my theory of the universe is that my relation to my own being and to the objective world is determined by reverence for life."[13]

Forty-eight years later Paul Andersen observed, "The philosophy of Aspen, as expressed by Schweitzer, was rooted firmly in humanitarian idealism, the same footing on which the Aspen Institute was founded to bring humanitarian values to businessmen. But we have hard, rocky ground in Aspen, and while the roots struggled for a hold, they never really took. That's why Schweitzer is largely forgotten here, as is the humanitarianism he espoused."[14]

In fact, Schweitzer's ideas were never understood. Reports from the two thousand people at the festival acknowledged that when Schweitzer spoke they were in such awe of his presence that they scarcely heard what he was saying.[15] They and Schweitzer were in two different worlds although they came together for a few days at the head of the Roaring Fork River valley. For decades Schweitzer had moved with reverence for all of his parts: mind, body, emotions and essence. Most

The light necessary to find the needed pathway can be developed only when the spirit is willing to learn, to know, and to grow.

- Page Bailey

In the stillness of the African jungle I have been able to work out this thought and give it expression.

- Albert Schweitzer

Americans have not made that integration. Most Americans do not have his wholeness. Schweitzer lived in a synergy of all his parts with the earth. He had already transcended the dilemma of fragmentation in which we dwell. He recognized that, "Descartes led modern philosophy astray by cutting the world up into objects (bodies) which have extension and objects (minds) which think, and then refusing to each of them the possibility of influencing the other." Schweitzer observed that Descartes believed "in a common neglect of nature. . ." and "overlooked the fact that she is living, and that she exists for her own sake. It is because he cannot join (Descartes) in this that Goethe dares to confess that he understands nothing about philosophy . . . overwhelmed by the mysterious individual life in nature, he (Goethe) adheres to a magnificently unfinished world-view. With the spirit of an investigator he looks into everything; in that of an inquirer he looks upon everything. He wants to think optimistically."[16] When Schweitzer stood in Aspen he was whole, he had not been led astray.

Schweitzer's "reverence for life" began with reverence for his own being and from this he extended reverence to all life. Chief Seattle said, "Every part of this earth is sacred to my people. Every single pine needle, every sandy shore, every mist in the dark woods, every meadow, every humming insect. All are holy in the memory and experience of my people." The value of "reverence for life" always rang true for me, but despite my respect for Schweitzer, living in reverence for life remained beyond my understanding and reach. Although I have had his books for forty years, his meaning and words came to life for me only with the teaching of an Apache, who told me, "You have a right to be a part of the whole." That concept slowly

You must speak straight so that your words may go as sunlight into our hearts.

- Cochise

and organically grew within me. The concept of 'right to be' is like the relationship between a tree and its root system. The roots are virtually unseen, but vital to the strength and well being of the tree. The 'right to be' cannot be seen, weighed or measured, but it has a profound effect upon the health and life of a person. As I began to claim my 'right to be' Schweitzer's words came alive. I had not been very observant for all of those years. I can't have reverence for others if I don't have reverence for myself. That Schweitzer included reverence for himself had gone unnoticed by me.

The concept of 'right to be' is central to lifestyle issues. Personal accountability has become a focus of medicine over the past twenty-five years because of its correlation with life-style-related illnesses and chronic conditions. The concept of a 'right to be' is fundamental to life style choices, for one must possess this first in order to engage in responsible self care. Because the phrase 'right to be' is not commonplace in this culture, one of the objectives of this book is to bring meaning to these words.

This 'right to be' concept is central to a paradigm of health. Health is not equated with medical care for the treatment of disease and injury. The current medical model is based on external authority rather than individual 'right to be' and self-responsibility.[17]

Inherent in the concept of 'right to be' is an alignment between the Creator and myself, which allows me now to see life from a place of reverence. Native Americans and Albert Schweitzer came from different perspectives, but they both knew a reverence for life. If they had ever had the opportunity, they could have understood this about each other, for they were hearing the

The natural world allows us to make peace with our own contradictory natures. We are returned to a balance of mind and spirit. We are healed.

- Terry Tempest Williams

I am saying society is based on shared meanings, which constitute the culture.

- David Bohm

*Mountains have
the power to
awaken an
overwhelming sense
of the sacred.*

- Edwin Bernbaum

same music. The music rising from them and from the earth was in harmony. It is joyful, sacred music.

For many years the sacred and the invisible were difficult for me. Like the roots of a tree, the sacred is unseen. Unless continuously acknowledged, it will fade from awareness. As I grew older, my essence dried up with living and competing in urban work arenas. But it came to life again outside in nature and in the presence of people who respected my sacredness. I have come to know that this quality is vital, and now under favorable conditions it can travel indoors with me. Some aspect of the invisible can become understandable. For example, our life is dependent upon unseen oxygen entering our body. I know this and have learned to give thanks. I can not see the ocean of invisible air flowing about me, but can indirectly read its manifestations in the changing clouds and moving leaves. I am changed when I understand and give thanks. Similarly, a reservoir of invisible sacred information is available from the Holy Spirit to my essence, if I invite it in and receive it with gratitude. The Hopi call the unseen powers, the Kachina, the spirit of invisible forces in life. My essence is not only invisible, but has been so often neglected, that I must continually remember to invite it to be with me. When I do that, it is possible to feel reverence for myself and the life around me. The concept has taken root in my being.

Schweitzer said, "I want to throw faith in a new humanity like a burning torch into our dark times."[18] For his words and the eloquent words of Native Americans to have an effect upon our intention, their meaning must penetrate our hearts, as well as our minds. When the meaning does take root and leap to life, it rises out of the earth through our whole being, taking a unique form in each of us.

There are many paths over the land.

> No one went yesterday
> Nor goes today
> Or will go tomorrow
> By this same path
> That I go
>
> For each person
> Holds inside a
> New ray of light
> From the sun . . and
> Has a virgin path
> To God
>   León Felipe

The transformation of people starts not through knowledge but through joy.

**- Torkom
Saraydarian**

Much of the time I will write in the first person. This is done with humility, it is the best way I know to share how my walk over the earth toward health has become a pilgrimage. It is done with humility, for I stand in awe and wonder before the mystery of it all. All of this sounds quite serious. But traveling with nature and 'the right to be' has a rhythm of activity and rest. There are playful and fun times on the journey, contained within the renewing cycle of joy.

CHAPTER 1

A Dream About What Might Have Been

Sometimes I am caught on a narrow path blocked by fear, where no options seem possible. My way isn't working. Then I go into a canyon, the woods, or up on to the ridge. In these quiet places inspiration and new options come to me. Once on the ridge a deep quiet surrounded me. I received a dream, a clear vision, of what might have been. It was a dream that went back in time, but from it flowed new understandings about today, and a vision of the future for tomorrow.

O! it is excellent
To have a giant's
strength,
but it is tyrannous
To use it like a giant.

- William
Shakespeare

The dream seemed to be set a hundred years ago and fear did not sweep down the valley of the Roaring Fork to the Colorado River. The Ute People had not yet been relocated. In fact, in my dream something altogether different from relocating them to reservations occurred. Different choices had been made about where and how they would be able to live. A different future began to unfold in Ute City during the 1870s and 1880s. This is how it went.

A Quaker man who had read an early draft of Helen Hunt Jackson's book, *A Century of Dishonor,* the classic account of our government's mistreatment of Native Americans, talked with a remittance man, who played polo with the Utes at Glenwood Springs. The Quaker loaned the book to the remittance man, who read it and returned it with a carefully scripted note. The note said, "I did not know! There were so many

16

promises broken. What can be done? How can I help?" The Quaker folded the note, put it in his coat pocket and turned to look up the valley. Deep inside, he knew that something could be done. He knew the power of one man, for he had been told the story of John Woolman, who lived in colonial America during the 1700s. In those times, Quakers owned slaves.

Over several decades, John Woolman had quietly talked with slave-holding Quakers sharing his view that the ownership of another human being was a violation of religious and human decency. When he was finished, Quakers did not own slaves, and Woolman had set the stage for the Quaker involvement in the Underground Railroad and the Civil Rights movements.[1]

I dreamed that day after day, these memories of Woolman moved through the body, emotions, heart, and mind of this Quaker man as he worked at the lumber mill. What could be done? Expansion, mining and ranching interests were pushing for the Utes to be "removed from the state." He traveled down valley and again found the remittance man and said, "If I did not have to work at the sawmill, I could go up to the mines and read to the men from this book at their meals and talk with the storekeepers and ranchers, before more people come. Then they too would know. There are very few of us here now, but soon many will be here. If anything can be done, now is the time." The remittance man said, "Yes, it can be done."

It was done. Quietly the Quaker read and talked with people, day after day. Enough understanding was established that agreement grew and the people spoke with clarity to the Governor, who said to Ouray, " The valley of the Roaring Fork River is part

That man's silence is wonderful to listen to.

- Thomas Hardy

*If there is magic
on this planet,
it is contained
in water.*

- Loren Eiseley

*....listen
This living flowing
land is all there is,
forever
We are it
it sings through us.*

- Gary Snyder

of your home land, but we have many more people than you. We want the silver metal and the coal deposits up the valley. We are taking the land on the right hand side of the river as we look upstream, but you, Utes, may continue to live on the left-hand side of the river up to the highest ridge, where you may keep your old ways. Stay north of the river."

"Both of us can take fish from the river, but we will not cross the Roaring Fork and Utes must never cross to this side." In my dream, the valley was divided, each side a separate domain. Because of the distinct differences between the two cultures, it was agreed that any exchanges or trading to be made between the two peoples must occur only on the ridges, to minimize contact and conflict. No bridges or hostilities were wanted. Unlike any other reservation, this agreement effectively shut down communication, except for a few traders. For a white man to encounter a Ute required traveling to Leadville and riding by horseback or walking up onto the ridges. The Ute numbers were small. Survival was more difficult than ever. They had lost access to the great healing hot springs where the Colorado and Roaring Fork come together, and were no longer able to migrate in winter to the warmer valleys downstream.

Minimal exchange and trading did go on. But the integrity of the Ute relationship to the land and the wholeness of their cultural ways survived. Across the valley there were no fences, no roads and no automobiles. No airplanes landed in their territory, because there were no landing strips. The people walked or rode horses, lived in wickiups or teepees and continued the ways and wisdom of living that had been passed to them through oral tradition from as long ago as any of their people could remember. Ouray and Chipeta had come to all of the councils that culminated in the successful agreement, and now lived with these Northern Ute people and brought a subtle influence of Apache ways.

On the south side of the river, the era of silver mining in Aspen ended, and until after the Second World War there were ranching, a little mining, and quiet years on the right side of the valley. In 1949 Albert Schweitzer was invited to the Goethe Bicentennial, an event to welcome Germany back into the family of nations after World War II. He spoke of "reverence for life." Skiing on Aspen Mountain was as fine as ever. Music filled the summer afternoons. Fred Braun and Stewart Mace built back country huts. In the 1950s growth and "development" of the right-hand side of the valley began to accelerate. The old post office gave way to Tom's Market on the corner of Hyman Avenue and Galena Street, which was in turn replaced by a succession of retail stores. Ranches became golf courses. Traffic on the highway increased and a four lane divided road was constructed to bring more people in faster. The highway was like another river in the valley carrying an increasing flow of vehicles and people upstream to Aspen.

On the other side of the river there was no such development. A small, but thriving community blended almost invisibly into the landscape. It is worthy of note that each person there was performing a function essential to this small community. Life was built on an understanding of and respect for the earth, its plants, creatures, land, air, and water. In this system no money changed hands. Rather, Ute prosperity and abundance depended upon cooperation and interdependence with each other and nature. Actions were

The mental illness of these times, as we approach the year 2000, comes from the idea that the invention, which is built by the hand, is more powerful than the person.

- Dhyani Ywahoo

carefully talked over in councils and dialogues. The children learned respect for and from their elders. The measure of a person's action was whether it was best for all concerned, including the individual himself, for the next seven generations.

In Aspen, Carbondale, and Glenwood Springs the "quiet years" passed, life and competition sped up. The relationship of work to living fast-forwarded to a focus on the increasing amount of money necessary to keep apace with modern technology. Life and travel accelerated, with more people working two and even three jobs to make an "adequate" income. Many traveled an hour or more per day to their employment. Consequences included social fragmentation of communities and families along with the adverse effects on the health of both young people and adults. The youth began to report that they did not feel valued by adults.

*There is beauty for
the ear in
the wilderness.*

- William O. Douglas

For years, the fishermen on both sides of the river recognized the contrasts between the two ways of life. Fishermen on the south bank observed that the Utes competed with each other in only their horse racing and their arts and crafts. Their fishing techniques were perceived to be primitive, but effective. However, the Utes were thought of as silly because they threw food to the fish. When questioned, they explained that it was a gift given in "thanks to the trout." Understanding grew over the years among generations of fisherman. They came to respect the Ute relationship with the earth and waters, the fish, the four-leggeds and the "wingeds" because they could see the abundant wildfowl and game. Despite centuries of Ute hunting, only on the north side of the river did mountain bison still run wild.

Climbers and a few physicians learned a little from the Ute medicine people and wisdom holders up on the peaks. The limited cultural exchange took on a new dimension when a few fisherman began to float the river in rafts in the 1950s. Later came kayakers, who were more maneuverable, and their numbers grew. Within this sub-population a significant shift in understanding began to occur. Enough contact developed with natives on the other shore that boaters started to report that the Utes, despite their "impoverished, primitive and difficult lifestyle," were a happy people who did not dwell in fear and scarcity. It was difficult for the Utes to understand that health and happiness on the other side of the river was most dependent upon money. But they had even more difficulty understanding how the minds of the people across the river were controlled by fear.

I dreamed that in the 1980s, when people came to realize this unique cultural situation, the Utes experienced international pressure from physicians, psychologists, and anthropologists who wanted to document and understand through scientific research "the unique Roaring Fork Ute tradition" which contrasted so strongly with other reservation Native Americans. One group of investigators were able to gain Ute cooperation. There was an overall shorter life expectancy for the Utes. However, the studies led to a remarkable finding, that the physical and mental health of young people in Aspen, the most affluent mountain community in North America, was not as good as that of the primitive youth living in isolation across the river.

A total of seven physical, mental, and culturally adapted indicators were used: 1) cardiovascular fitness, 2) body fat, 3) meaningful life purpose, 4) sense of coherence index, 5) stress management skills, 6)

Nature is one of the languages that God speaks.

- **Robert Bly**

emotional intelligence and stability, 7) intergenerational relationship index. The Ute numbers were small, but statistically significant. When the report was published in the New England Journal of Medicine (NEJM) other researchers and computer programmers insisted that the Ute medicine people cooperate in developing software to aid counselors in dealing with deteriorating American family and social relationships and help in the promotion of asset development for young people. The pressure was too much and the wisdom holders withdrew from the ridges and could no longer be found at the river bank. The NEJM report generated not only controversy, but also curiosity. How could the Utes possibly have healthier young people? They had no modern educational system, medical care, or technology and apparently no interest in adapting these modern ways. But the Utes no longer greeted visitors. No one was invited for a hospitable meal in a Ute campsite.

In my dream nevertheless, the remarkable story of Ute health and wisdom continued to unfold slowly. In 1997, a kayaker who had defected returned after nine years on the other shore. Because of his affinity for the water he had been known as Ouzel by the local boaters. The name came from the aquatic bird known more properly as the dipper, *Cinclus mexicanus unicolor,* which dives and swims under water to obtain insects, crustaceans and small fishes. The bird received its name from the habit of bobbing or dipping up and down on the rocks in the water. Ouzel was named by his school friends, to whom he was most familiar when he was grinning and bobbing up and down in his kayak on a favorite stretch of the Roaring Fork River. For years, it had been known that a few kayakers never came back. But Ouzel did return and reported respect for the Ute culture and could explain some of the psycho-social fac-

To understand the meaning of the whole - and that is what a world view demands! - is for us an impossibility.

- **Albert Schweitzer**

tors that contributed to the hardiness of their health. For over a decade, a small number of experienced boaters climbed out on the other shore. Ouzel had a reputation as an able kayaker. Those who knew him before his defection to Ute territory described Ouzel as a young man who had a oneness with the river. But as they observed him, people would say "Now, Ouzel is always at one with himself," for this presence was with him everywhere and not limited to the river. They did not know how else to describe him; it was as if he were on the water when he was talking with a group of seventh graders about how mountain asters are an interdependent community. After his return, when people would ask him what he experienced as the most significant change within himself, Ouzel said, "Over there I came to understand what Albert Schweitzer meant when he spoke about 'reverence for life'." At that, people's heads would spin around, a startled look would spread across their face. They did not understand.

Ouzel would add, "Now, I am working cooperatively with all of my parts. The first thing I learned from the Utes was respect for myself and for them. It changed the meaning of my life. What I feel is as normal as water flowing down the valley. It is life moving through me." People could see he had serenity and vitality. But they expected him to talk about hunting with spears, wearing buckskins and sleeping under bear robes. Often they would say to him, "Ouzel these feelings you describe are not rational!" He would smile and wink, "That's right, there is nothing rational about feelings, there isn't supposed to be." This didn't help, people had lots of questions about what he was saying.

The two questions he was asked most often were,

The discipline of seeing interrelationships gradually undermines older attitudes of blame and guilt.

- **Peter Senge**

*We thought,
because we had
power,
we had
wisdom.*

**- Stephen Vincent
Benet**

"Why did you go to the Ute side?" and "What was it really like?" The reason he went over was a surprise to many people. "My life had become running bigger and bigger rapids. Everyone expected me to do it, and no one would give me the space to acknowledge my fear. The Utes accepted me for who I am, including my fear. They did not care anything about my kayaking. Despite the hardship of their life, every person over there is valuable. Everyone contributes. They have a different way of speaking, seeing, and relating," he said. "Everyone over there claims their right to be a part of the community—all belong. Their relationships are not just with people, but with all of creation. They speak to each other with respect, not only in councils, but in everyday conversation. They see the strengths and talents of their children, and encourage them with blessing and affirmation, rather than controlling them by fear or shaming. Old people, kids, hunters and new mothers do everything together. It is the most amazing dance of cooperative intergenerational relationships I have ever seen. Everyone over there is certain, of their purpose, even the elderly. What we can learn from them is not about beadwork, feathers, and buckskin, it is about a healthy way to relate to yourself, to each other, and to the earth. We will never go back to where they are, but we can learn from them how to be more conscious as we go forward."

Then Ouzel would pause and look to see whether the person he was talking with was still with him. If they were, he would continue, "You know we joke about the fact that in Aspen the only thing that's sacred is money? Well, over there the creatures, people, earth, water—everything actually is sacred. The way they speak, the way they see, and the way they relate is with respect. Their way is healthy for them. They have reverence for all life. They taught me that I have a 'right to be.' I have reverence for myself and reverence for you." With this, some people would look away. But those who took in the concept began to change. Ouzel reported that the most striking transition he saw since leaving Aspen was the pace of life in the valley. "I knew the Utes were in a different time zone, but I am certain you people are going faster than when I left. The rhythm of life for the Utes is the rhythm of the earth, the roots of their health are in the earth. They have their problems, but life is calmer there. Despite its difficulties, life for them is not a continual crises."

Health indicators on the right-hand shore had been collected at focus groups by the Healthy Communities Initiative and were virtually all economic. Hourly wage, housing, commuting time to work, cost of living and doctors visits and hospitalization were the health concerns expressed by most people. They might sit and listen to Ouzel the kayaker, for a time, but they could not see how any of his experiences or stories could be helpful or relevant to them and their immediate needs. A few environmentally conscious people were becoming concerned with water quality because of the herbicides and chemicals being used by golf courses and a few ranchers to control the growing epidemic of houndstooth and burdock root weeds. But most of the valley neither knew nor cared.

However, Ouzel saw positive things happening which he found encouraging. Trends that he observed in Western Colorado—activities which he knew were components of a healthy community. There were people who were realizing that their opportunity and 'right to be' was something special and a sacred birthright. To those aware that they possess this wondrous gift, there was no longer any possibility that

Running water is a holy thing.

- Old Somerset saying

*There is a point of
correspondency between
two views which is
called the pivot of the
Tao. As soon as one
finds this pivot, he
stands in the center
of the ring of thought
where he can respond
without end to the
changing views;
without end to those
affirming, and
without end to
those denying.*

- Chang Tzu

they could believe that their purpose in life was merely to be a consumer. But, as technology accelerated the Utes were perceived as even more of an aberration. Many people assumed that they would not survive much longer, because they didn't have access to the "internet."

One of the encouraging signs Ouzel had observed was happening downstream in a medium sized Colorado community where "dialogue" had been going on for several years. Dialogue has its roots in the ancient tradition of council, where one person speaks at a time. This creates a safer mode of communication than competitive discussion which can often become confrontational. Ouzel had experienced council with the Utes and knew the modern form of "dialogue" could help to heal the disease of isolation and disconnection separating people in the Roaring Fork Valley and every other community he encountered. He knew part of the Ute success was the way they spoke to each other with respect. Ouzel saw those characteristics in the modern form of dialogue. He also saw it in the valley in the "conflict resolution work" which a woman named Barbe Chamblis had been doing in the form of council.

The second encouraging sign was that more groups were beginning to look at the strengths and talents of people, in preference to focusing exclusively on what was wrong with them. These people promoted resiliency and assets and were working with youth in communities all over the country. Resiliency is the positive capacity of an at-risk population to succeed despite adversity. The devaluation of youth, as experienced by young people in Aspen, Basalt, Crested Butte, Telluride, and Vail was, in fact, everywhere. People in Aspen were beginning to notice a program sweeping across the country called "Developmental

Assets," factored powerfully in shaping health, by reducing negative behavior and increasing positive actions in youth. There was also a successful program in Glenwood Springs for adults with chronic conditions, who learned to guide their nervous systems toward "Recovering."

The third encouraging sign Ouzel noticed was that programs for bringing different generations back into relationship with each other were springing up at the grassroots level across the nation. Mentors and elders were seeking to heal the gaps between young and old. Ouzel knew the components existed in his culture to claim key methods the Utes used to maintain a healthy community. What was necessary was to bring these together into a coherent whole. A potential existed for developing a model of health, founded on the 'right to be,' yet fear and greed were also present and powerful. People were face to face with the difficulty of the human spirit. Would the evolution of modern life be accompanied by an evolution of spirit? Could a container be built strong enough to hold health in the Roaring Fork Valley?

But this was only a dream. This dream of the Utes and Ouzel is not real. Utes do not dwell across the river from Aspen. We have a medical system, but no model of health. Nowhere on this continent do native people live in full cultural integrity with the earth of their ancestors. In fact, because they don't, their health suffers greatly because their souls are not moving in harmony with the soul of their homeland. Studies do not show their health to be better than other Americans.

However, if this dream called to you about a healing

The wholeness of life has, from of old, Been made manifest in its parts; Clarity has been made manifest in heaven, Firmness in earth, Purity in spirit,....

- Lao Tzu

*We must use a
twofold measure:
intention on the
one hand and response
on the other.*

- David Cooper

relationship with yourself, others, the Creator, and the earth—your future may involve building cooperation and bridges with reverence. You may choose to build a cooperative personal bridge from medicine to health, and do what Ouzel learned to do, claim your 'right to be a part of the whole.' Because analytical methods separate and disconnect whole beings and systems, bridging can be healing. Aborigines have always known, as Hawaiian kahunas have known, the dream of our future is sacred and malleable.[2] Do we intend to create a future of health and wholeness? Do we have an intention to make possible a positive and significant future for our children?

Some people believe it is now possible to re-integrate wisdom into our intention for the future.

CHAPTER 2

THE GIFT OF LIFE

Storm after storm
Snowflake after flake after flake
Settles onto the ridges and into the valleys
Along the continental divide

With spring
The earth turns its axis
To the sun
Now high in the sky

Snow melts into trickles flowing
Down from the dark blue high country
Rushing together into the earth's arteries
Vibrating the gorges as it roars

The water descends and seeds stir
New shoots of green life rise
From the meadows and the hillsides
Health pushes up as naturally as the springtime.

He not busy being born is busy dying.

- Bob Dylan

My father suffered from a chronic condition that made him ever careful of the food he ate and the pace he kept. He sought health from various practitioners, diets, and medications. He visited clinics, hot springs, and health spas. Because of his condition, an aura of fear was in our home and especially at the kitchen table where we sat for meals. He was always anxious about whether his body would tolerate the food he ate. But his healing occurred beside the flowing waters of the Roaring Fork, Crystal, and Frying Pan rivers. Beside them, as a fisherman, my father found joy and renewal. By healing, I mean he became whole and experienced peace of mind. The best measure of health is the ability of all our parts and systems to cooperatively work together. His body, mind, emotions, and essence came to a fully functioning agreement about the activity of fishing.

His chronic illness was not cured, but he made an alliance with his fear and pain that reduced his suffering. After the spring runoff was past, when the streams were low and clear, he could catch rainbow and brook trout with dry flies, and there was no time then for self-pity or suffering. His reconnection with nature was more meaningful than the illness. Whether the fishing was successful or not, my father had known from his youth a healing relationship with rivers. A good catch could be shown as a tangible measure of success. But totally apart from landing and cooking the fish, something in the process was healing for him. Seeking the trout was rewarding whether or not he caught a single fish, and he would repeat the process whenever given the opportunity. He never asked to understand how this occurred when he went into nature; he never sought to analyze it. Rather, he seized the opportunity whole. He knew that something powerful, though intangible, came to him there and all that was necessary was to receive it and give thanks.

My father had found his way to recognize and honor the gift of life. Each of us possesses this gift, but few of us treat it as a gift, as something we can use as well or as poorly as we choose. Our initial insight in claiming health comes from recognizing life as a gift. Other insights follow from this first one. When we recognize life as a gift we take a step toward acknowledging and balancing the wholeness of our connection with

Being in touch with fire and passion seems to be an essential need for the soul of a human being.

- David Whyte

nature, our desire to feel blessed rather than shamed, and our intense pleasure in joining our purpose to meaningful actions in our daily tasks and relationships. You cannot give what you have not received. Because my father had received and known the gift of a healing relationship with nature he was able to offer it to me. I seized it. Each day, I give thanks that he took me to the rivers, valleys, forests, and ridges.

Wholeness and Health

The English word "health" means "wholeness" and "to heal" means "to make whole."[1] Health is a cooperative process of all our parts and relationships acting to maintain meaningful function and a sense of coherence in the face of change in ourselves and our environment.[2] Healing is not about whether you die, but rather how fully you live.[3] Sometimes we travel with the directness and swiftness of an arrow in flight in order to fulfill our needs. Sometimes we seek in the larger circles and rhythms of nature and life to become part of a purpose greater than our individual needs. In both cases, clear intention and commitment are necessary. Seeking health requires the intention to integrate our personal and individual selves with larger processes. My father was able to receive the power that resides in our relationship with the earth. When we become a part of nature and a community greater than our own self, we become part of the whole.

Wholeness is inclusive of everything. It is not exclusive, but all embracing. The sky, earth, waters, and all creatures contribute to and take from the whole. Our wholeness is all parts of the self: mind, body, emotions, and essence functioning together. Being whole

We are no longer isolated individuals in conflict with our surroundings; we are parts of a whole, elements in a universal harmony.

- Bede Griffiths

is being a participant in the cyclic circle of life. The circle of life includes: health, disease, illness, injury, and death. Health care and medical care are a part. Wholeness has everything to do with relevance. Wholeness is the acceptance that you have the choice of meaningful relevance and must make the decision of what part you will play. What do you want to pay attention to? Wholeness is recognizing all that you are now without being distracted by all that you have been. To be whole is to know and claim "your right to be." As we become whole it is unnecessary to project chaos on ourselves or one another, unnecessary to intentionally manipulate, confuse, or create unnecessary fear.[4]

Few of us are able to do this. More often we see separation than wholeness, but when we begin to respect our own wholeness, we begin to heal. Fear can block our ability to receive the gift. But we are already part of the whole unconditionally, with strengths as well as infirmities, regardless of our fears. Wholeness does not know how to communicate that we are strange or flawed or frail. We are part of the whole as we are. This is what my father experienced when be chose to become part of the rivers and valleys. He accepted his relevance and experienced healing in participating with that part of the whole which was meaningful to him. The mountain streams did not judge him because of his chronic illness or fear.

Many are searching for a route to healing. Because the business of surviving today has become confusing and financially expensive, the journey of life can be making money. Meaning in life can be sought in fulfilling the function of being a consumer. Relevance can be measured by what you buy, wear, or drive. Yet many of us hunger for a more meaningful purpose, as

The greatest beauty is organic wholeness, the wholeness of life and things, the divine beauty of the universe. Love that, not man apart from that...

- Robinson Jeffers

well as enough financial success to survive. Many of us hunger to integrate life and work, the sacred and ordinary with the beautiful and practical. Where we spend the most time and where this is the most challenging is in our vocation. Our life's work is an expression of our essential self. We expand or contract according to whether we fill out and grow in our work or withdraw and shrivel.

My father expanded and became joyful as a fisherman, but shrank in the stress of his work as a salesman. Work is the opportunity to share acts of love and beauty. Life and work are not separate.[5] A Gallup Poll conducted some years ago identified the number one spiritual goal is to have a life with meaning and purpose. What lies beneath that desire? Beneath that desire is a deep understanding and need to not only take from the whole but give back to it. Inherent in meaningful work is what we give in exchange for what we take. If we only take, we leave a hole in the circle and experience the consequences of that imbalance.

With each step on the journey to health we move toward relevance and healing, or we receive a wound that travels through our being. We are blessed or we are shamed. Our need is to search for ways to integrate all our parts with each other, as well as, to the whole that surrounds us. This carries us toward wisdom about healing rather than toward accepting wounds. A healthy being is always seeking balance.[6]

Work and Health

The journey to health begins with the first movements of each new day. The work that a society chooses to do or not to do, defines its values and shapes its future.

If he is indeed wise he does not bid you enter the house of his wisdom, but rather leads you to the threshold of your own mind.

- Kahil Gibran

Because we work most of our waking lives, if we value life, we must consider what are we working for?[7] Work is a pivotal health moment, more predictive of heart disease than our cholesterol levels or blood pressure. If thinking of your work brings you satisfaction, you are indeed blessed, and your health is better for it.

Only when I claim a meaningful purpose and line my life and essence up with my gifts, do I have the balance and stability from which to support the development and diversity of my children, mate, colleagues, and community.

Physicians have a saying about properly identifying and diagnosing a disease state: "If you don't think to look for it, you won't find it." In this case, what you search and look for will influence what you do with your life, what you will become, what your goals will be, and the vision with which you see the process of living. If you never seek meaningful purpose, it will never be found. "Illness is guaranteed if mindbody lacks purpose or meaning."[8] Meaningless work is dangerous to your health. Whereas "meaning makes a great many things endurable—perhaps everything."[9]

Nothing in life is more meaningful than a sense of contribution and value. Purpose functions within the circle of relationships, family, and community, but it emanates from the inner sacredness of your right to be a part of the whole. Your sense of coherence in life depends on knowing and claiming who you are. It is a great loss when our vision becomes focused only on what someone else wants or what is wrong, for then we may fail to see and activate our unique beauty and talents. What a loss when we fail to find our place to fill as a useful and conscious contributor. Just as a muscle becomes deconditioned and weak with lack of

Employment is nature's physicisn, and is essential to human happiness.

- Galen

We are continually hiding our light under a bushel because we feel safest that way.

- David Whyte

To some extent, while we think we are simply driving to work every morning to earn a living, the soul knows it is secretly engaged in a life-or-death struggle for its existence.

- David Whyte

use, our capacities and talents shrivel and weaken if we do not use them. "Purpose becomes vague when you no longer act on purpose."[10] But "how impressive to see what people can do when they cease to focus upon what they cannot do!"[11]

Meaningless work can be painful and is characterized by an absence of joy. Without joy a person becomes lazy and unwilling to strive and labor. The absence of joy makes a person arrogant, insensitive, uncooperative, stubborn, and mentally closed.[12] If you are dissatisfied with your job, your trip to work carries with it more than the absence of joy. Work dissatisfaction is the strongest predictor known for heart disease, low back disability, and repetitive motion disorders. Since 1973, the Department of Health and Human Services has known that the strongest indicator for heart disease is not smoking, hypertension, high cholesterol or diabetes mellitus but job dissatisfaction.[13] "Meaning is physically active."[14] Work dissatisfaction can manifest physically. "Unexpressed creativity is painful."[15] In fact, disability because of low back pain, a major medical and economic problem in this country, has a stronger statistical relationship to job dissatisfaction than to the physical demands of the work.[16] When meaning is not acknowledged but disability is, there is a movement toward creating more disability. In other words, the meaning your work has for you is significant, healthy or unhealthy. Larry Dossey, MD, has written extensively on meaning and medicine. He observes, the medical system largely denies meaning as an important factor in illness in the belief that it is scientific to do so.[17]

The importance of job satisfaction to your health is known to physicians, employers, politicians, and labor leaders, but we lack a coherent understanding of this

We simply spend too much time and have too much psychic and emotional energy invested in the workplace for us to declare it a spiritual desert bereft of life giving water.

- David Whyte

*We are all aware of
how work both
embodies us and
strangles our soul
life in the very
same instant.*

- David Whyte

*A soulful approach to
work is probably the
only way an
individual can respond
creatively to the high
temperature stress of
modern work life
without burning to
a crisp in the heat.*

- David Whyte

truth that has translated into effective treatment. There is no American Medical Association map, strategy, or proposal telling you how to make your work meaningful. In your work you are a case of one. Modern physicians and medical technology offer few if any helpful recommendations. The notable exception to the void of medical support for your purpose was Albert Schweitzer, who advised, "The only way to further the brotherhood of man is to fulfill one's duty completely." He was speaking of a commitment to the whole. When individual purpose and vision connect with something larger than ourselves power and vision expand. Peter Senge observes, "Individuals committed to a vision beyond their self-interest find they have energy not available when pursuing narrower goals."[18]

But today the problem of job satisfaction for most workers challenges so many facets of the American way that its perceived complexity has deflected all planning and therapeutic efforts. Receiving a salary is often the compensation we are given for forgetting who we are.[19] You may be a victim of disempowering corporate policies or lack of medical or political insight, but to do so you must first agree to give away reverence for your own life and value, your "right to be part of the whole." In fact, the answer is straightforward. But it is not an easy answer or path. The courage to find meaningful work satisfaction is a solo journey made by only a few. A recent national survey found 95 percent of people dissatisfied with their vocation.[20] Many desire work that fills spiritual as well as material needs but the way is difficult. In modern life "we desperately need—an awareness of the sacred in the ordinary."[21] Meaningful purpose rises directly from our essence.

The opportunity to choose relevant and meaningful work is a gift that can lead to the blessing of healing. This opportunity is more available to us than to our parents or grandparents. My father, who grew up in the Great Depression, once said to me, "It is wonderful that you ask about what work you will do and your purpose, because I never had the opportunity—I got a job and worked to survive." Those of us now living in North America are the first large group of people in the history of time free to become what our essence has coded us to be. However, our choices and our inertia often block this opportunity. Rarely is the opportunity blocked solely because we have no choice.[22] We can allow our inventions and technology to become diversions and distractions that obstruct the full unfolding of our being and purpose. Or we can use them as the means and tools to create rewarding and satisfying labor. A relevant contribution to the whole. When a gathering of such individuals make this commitment, whole communities or organizations can experience the energy of a growing process.

A Challenging Journey

This journey to health is not simple. Seeking to get anywhere requires the choice of a viable route. Nature will screen out the unfit and uncommitted. If you intend to embark upon the quest for health it will take you over a challenging landscape of evolving conditions. It will be more than a trip to the market to pick up a new vitamin supplement. There are dangers and pitfalls along the way. Some will say following the rules is the key to finding the path, and there is truth in this. There is much to be learned from the experienced and wise. Science can help us to measure the hazards of smoking cigarettes and the adverse effects

It must always be remembered that embarking on any path of personal growth is a matter of choice.

- Peter Senge

of consuming excessive amounts of alcoholic beverages. Studies confirm the benefits of a high fiber, low cholesterol diet for most of the population. But objective guidelines do not exist for fitting individual strengths and weaknesses with a sacred way of living that leads to a meaningful life purpose. Seeking health is necessarily an individual path and process. Inner wisdom and judgment are as important as general principles. Therefore, both your own awareness of what you know and feel, as well as competent guidance from chosen allies and teachers will give vital help on the journey. Unconscious ignorance increases the risks. Total commitment is necessary, a half hearted effort will not get you there.

The journey will involve overcoming barriers and obstacles and threading through a forest of paradox and conflict, but in places you will reach vantage points, and locate bridges over the chasms of fear, grief, anger, and doubt. Honoring these places will help you use these connections of insight and transformation to link your life with meaning and purpose. By moving unconsciously we may step over a jewel laying upon our path, but if we are awake and aware the moment can be seized, the significance can be honored and the value consciously integrated. There will be times for action and speaking as well as times for listening and stillness. Periods of uncertainty will be inevitable, and struggle will be an inherent part of finding the way. Confidence is wonderful, but arrogance is dangerous. Boldness is necessary, but carelessness never is.

Following our path is in effect a kind of going off the path, through open country. There is a certain early stage when we are left to camp out in the wilderness alone, with few supporting voices.

- David Whyte

Regaining Ancient Wisdom

The journey to health need never extend far from

home. Still, increasingly many of us leave this safety as we hasten through complex schedules, commuting, and travel. We speed through crowds of strangers, in contrast to our ancestors who traveled short distances, largely among neighbors. For the most part their communities held a greater calmness than ours because they had a natural harmony between labor and movement, just as a flight of swallows turning above the water or a herd of caribou grazing over the tundra has a grace that comes from being part of nature.

From out in space, the earth is a blue and green sphere. The blue is the water and the green is the plants, alive with healthy movement, in contrast with our current unhealthy ways. The manual work of the past was hard and heavy, but it was a valid exchange with nature. We have replaced that work with a mechanical order and structure necessary to control the speed of modern living, production, and travel. As a result we have created urban concentrations of discord. These centers contrast with the grace we can see in nature when we take the time to watch animals move with harmony over the earth, a movement which supports their health and 'right to be a part of the whole.' Our ancestors were part of this whole and were able to listen to the wisdom of our fellow creatures and of plants. Today, however, many of us have left the path of health and have lost our connection to the whole.

There is an ancient Chinese saying that the greatest gift of life is life itself. A seed that holds this gift can survive for long periods until conditions become favorable. It holds the necessary information and potential for life in reserve, in dormancy, sometimes for years until the right moment. One day the sprout hidden

Of all the elements, the Sage should take Water as his preceptor. Water is yielding, but all conquering. Water extinguishes fire, or finding itself likely to be defeated, escapes as steam and reforms.......

**- Tao Cheng
11th Century AD**

The sacred call enters our heart's secret cavity, evoking an awareness that eclipses our normal daily experience, attuning us to a new level of appreciation.

- David Cooper

within breaks forth. With sufficient moisture and fire from the sun the seed begins to pull in water, to grow and swell, pushing a green stalk upward toward the light as it pushes roots downward following the flow of living liquid. The gift within breaks through the dark soil and bursts into the sunshine to become a participant in the field of plants around it.

A seed contains enough food for the gift of life to begin its movement. But not until the plant establishes a successful interdependence with surrounding sources of support is healthy life able to continue. Whether a seed is to become a blade of grass or a mighty redwood tree, it must choose life with sufficient strength and intention to withstand heat and cold and drought and storm, to take nourishment from the soil and blend it with sunlight and gases from the air. This is the wisdom of a total commitment to living that was available to our ancestors, as it is to us. If we listen.

Sense of coherence contributes to health by influencing an individual's ability to cope with stressors successfully. If the coping process is unsuccessful, the tension aroused by the stressor is transformed into pathogenic stress.

- Aaron Antonovsky

In order to become a flower, plant, or tree, the seed is destroyed. It is transformed. Germination is an explosion in which the unified body of the seed vanishes and becomes the root and stem.[23] One place I heard this wisdom was in the garden. I wanted to grow cucumbers, and because the plot was small, I constructed a frame for the vines to grow vertically. To support the frame I cut a straight bare stake from a nearby willow bush. It was about five feet long, and I pushed it a foot into the ground to anchor the frame. One evening a month later, my wife and I were in the garden, when she called, "Look at this. A tree is growing among the cucumbers." Indeed, several new branches with a dozen bright green leaves extended out and upward from the straight stake. A garden is always extraordinary as new life comes out of the earth, but now the wonder of the garden was even greater.

The occasion led me to recall walking the bank the Frying Pan River as a child, beside my father. We crossed over a fence with posts cut from aspen trees. There, too, the posts were growing new branches and leaves. The wisdom of the garden was passed to a new generation when my children came to look. Awed by the new leaves on the stick, they said, "The dead branch has come back to life." Like the garden, life and death, illness and healing are a part of the movement of the whole. Seeking health and purpose is a wondrous journey of claiming a place in the whole and finding a path to relevance.

Even though a plant may seem simple to us, it is a sensitive and complex being from which we can learn much about healthy living. In the presence of sunshine, chlorophyll in the plant's leaves produces sugar, and the plant uses the sugar to grow not only in size but complexity. Its will to persevere and to stand with an identity and presence is so strong that it can grow even in unlikely and inhospitable cracks in a rock or crevices in a mountain. Nature supports and nourishes life with a harmonious web of interdependent systems, a unified field that resembles a functional human community. For example, as long as a plant lives it shares with us the vital gift of oxygen. We give back to it the carbon dioxide it needs. From the beginning of our life on this planet there has been this exchange. The community of plants transforms the energy of the sun into food for us and the animals of the earth. Life takes strength from life in continuous interlocking cycles, and gives back to the whole as our ancestors knew, who moved with these rhythms. Giving and taking is a flow of reciprocity essential to health.

But the plant also faces inevitable challenges that

Our lives are like a candle in the wind.

- **Carl Sandburg**

*The needles of the pine
All to the west incline.*

**- Henry David
Thoreau**

*Within and around
the earth, within
and around the hills,
within and around
the mountains, your
authority returns
to you.*

- A Tewa Prayer

question whether it will survive. If water, sunshine, soil with the right nutrients, or air containing sufficient carbon dioxide stops being available, the plant will die. Similarly, people suffer illness and death when their basic life needs are not met. Yet we need more than air, water, and food to survive healthfully. Among these basic needs are many that are within our choice. We can make healthy adaptations to life's challenges, just as the cypress tree does on the coast as it is twisted by the prevailing wind from the sea. Or as the bristle-cone pine that grows at timberline does by growing its needles on the sheltered side of its branches. Even a simple squash blossom in a garden adapts and turns toward the sun, manifesting one of the attributes of life: spontaneous movement and self-organization. There is a relationship between health and a relevant and successful response to a challenge. A meaningful purpose supports survival.

Plants show us something else significant if we take the time to look. A group of mountain asters can live together cooperatively. Each plant takes water and nourishment from the earth and sky, but does not attack another. A family of mountain asters extend the 'right to be' to one another, this acceptance has much to teach us about community. Their roots in the earth are closely interdependent. Aspen trees offer an additional perspective. Each tree grows from the roots of its neighbor. A hillside of aspen trees is actually one family in community.

The meaning and teaching of plants was a type of wisdom known to Schweitzer. He in fact used plant images when speaking about the importance of gratitude, reciprocity, and thankfulness. "Certain plants in nature spread below the earth. The root grows in the soil and sends up shoots at intervals so that eventually several plants are standing near one another, apparently independent and unconnected. Yet in reality they all came from a common root that existed at the start. That is how your deeds of kindness should spread. Let the kindness you receive send out fertile roots from which new plants may grow. You must learn to understand the secret of gratitude, for it is more than what we call a virtue. Learn to see it as a mysterious law of existence. In obedience to it we have to fulfill our destiny."[24]

Blessing and the Right to Be

A child is conceived. From the union of a man and a woman comes a single cell that carries the double twisting information strands of life, the genetic code. This creation is surrounded by the mother's being and womb, bathed in a harmony of nourishment. At nine months the infant is born, draws in air, and sends out its first sound. This initial breath is the first universal action of all children as they become part of the world outside their mother. It is our primal connection with the unified field of nature. At death, releasing the last breath releases that connection. But how do we become conscious and live as full participants of the whole between our first and last breaths?

I will bless those who bless you.

- Genesis 12:3

Schweitzer believed that reverence for life is the "source of constant renewal for the individual and for mankind."[25] The birth of a child is the gift and renewal of human life. When we give thanks and acknowledge the gift with gratitude, we prepare the infant for life as a relevant member of the whole. Conditions for an infant, as for a seed, must be favorable, or at least adequate, if the beauty of full growth and development is to occur. We humans require not only a long

*Blessed is he who
blesses you.*

- Numbers 24:9

period of gestation but, much more than any other species, prolonged years of careful nurturing, to fully mature. We need physical nourishment and protection. We also need a more subtle level of safety if we are to develop not only physically but mentally, emotionally, and spiritually, in order to develop receptive minds and hearts and later healthy interdependence and relationships. Although ours is not a culture of the heart, parents and community can still give conscious thanks for the gift of a child's birth, acknowledging the child's wholeness, and appreciating a greater power than themselves.

If this thanking is joined with blessing of the child's essence and potential, the soul of the child, as well as his ego may be acknowledged and nourished in growth. For many of us the rigors of competition and the shaming we endure as we grow are challenging, as was the difficulty of physical labor for our ancestors. While it is never too late to feel blessed rather than shamed in our lives, we must make that our intention. We fulfill our own journey toward being blessed when we bless our children. What do I mean by being blessed? A blessing invokes balance, wholeness, and divine favor on the right of a child to be a relevant participant of the whole. The family and community who bless all of the child: mind, body, emotions, essence, and purpose; affirm their love and belief in this being. You can learn to bless, only if you know that you are blessed. You cannot give that which you do not have, so if you are to offer a blessing you must have first received one yourself. You must have accepted it, in order to be able to give it.

The antithesis of my 'right to be' is no right to be. With no right to be I feel shame. The opposite of being blessed is being shamed.[26] "Shame is a sudden severing from the world."[27] It is that act or action that separates us from our cultural group. Shame takes place in a social context.[28] The shame position is one from which I no longer acknowledge myself as worthy of a social position.[29] Shame is distinguished from healthy guilt which teaches us a lesson and has positive value. Being shamed means I am no good, there is something wrong with me. This is worse than irrelevance. "Shame, says I am a mistake . . . It is total non-self acceptance . . . Shame is a kind of soul murder."[30]

Shame happens when we permit it to happen. It is a condition that can be avoided by denying the shame position. If the culture is holding the shame in place, you may need to release the culture. Do not let the mindbody become a shame multiplier. Because shame can dominate the nervous system.[31] Shame is the negative thought that denies our positive potential. It is so negative a force that it literally invalidates us.

Without affirmation, without blessing and reverence for my being, I seek approval for what I do. Approval for the clothes I wear, the car, the house, and the work. But unless these satisfy me at the core. I still hunger for affirmation of my right to be. My clothes, my car, my house, my work are not enough. I want more. I want a new one. A more technologically advanced one, only the latest model will do it. The media is at my fingertips to suggest the new one that will make me happy.

But when I have a 'right to be a part of the whole,' when I know that I am sacred, I can recognize how much is enough and that nature surrounds me with abundance. When I am nourished by the infinite abundance of the universe, it is possible to make an alliance with fear and no longer be driven into a fren-

*shame is...
... a sickness
of the soul.*

- Gershen Kaufman

A negative thought is a thought which denies access to a real and positive potential for action, experience or achievement that would otherwise be available.

- Page Bailey

zy by the anxiety of scarcity. With knowing enough, I can separate my needs from my wants. With a blessing from my community I am able to learn to guide my nervous system so that my mindbody and emotions cooperate with my essence. It doesn't just happen. We have to talk and negotiate. Mind says, "I want to be in control." Body says, "I want to be warm, comfortable and well feed." Emotions say, "I want to be happy. Ever-changing feelings are flowing through me continuously." Essence says, "Don't forget me, I am immortal, I receive the Holy Spirit." These parts dialogue and learn from each other. Increasingly we come together and are able to cooperate in actions which would have been previously blocked by conflict or fear. Essence, my soul, when connected to the whole of creation is renewed. Whenever I take time to say hello to my essence, it speaks to me with a glow of joy. Healing is in my sacredness not in shame.

Meaning changes as our understanding changes.

- Page Bailey

The quality of a child's relationship with her parents and community is fundamental to the development of her mind, body, emotions, and essence. This relationship will influence the child's attitudes and awareness about learning and future relationships. It will affect her health. Being blessed is the most important ingredient for a child's growth and health. Blessing affirms a child's value. It is the soil in which the child's purpose and contribution back to people will take hold and grow. With giving a blessing a cycle of reciprocity is carried forward. For that child will give to the community and be able to extend a blessing to the next generation. A balanced cycle of giving and taking is supported.

A positive thought is a thought which gives us full access to a real and positive potential for action, experience or achievement

- Page Bailey

As a child I was fortunate to have a doctor who cared for me with medical remedies but who also blessed me, with words and actions which recognized my 'right to be.' A reverence for my life was affirmed. Dr. MacDonald radiated a joyfulness that was healing whenever I was in his presence, and I recognized at an early age that he knew the way to health. Whenever I got sick he was able to heal me, whether it was with a word of reassurance, a touch of his hand, a pill, or an injection. He was a blesser, a healer, and a pediatrician. I am certain that he saw all children and the entire world as he saw me. He extended to each of us the fullness of his joy in living. Having been in his presence, I never doubted that I would grow up to be someone who would contribute to a community.

As we mature, our physical growth, function, and regulation follow the directions of the DNA in each of our cells. Our minds and souls follow our experience to grow and evolve throughout our lives, but this can be arrested in fear at any point and close down. Our minds and souls as well as our bodies need nourishment and schooling from family, community, and nature to continue the process of growth toward health.

Developing Wholeness

The first need of the child's mind is to sense safety for himself in order, to establish a balance of trust over mistrust.[32] This safety zone is where our individual 'right to be' is rooted. It is the base from which we mark our boundaries. This is a critical time in the child's development, when he looks into your eyes with complete trust. The child can be nourished by your teaching and blessing, and grow with a mind as radiant as the sun. Or she can be cursed by fear, anger, or shaming to develop a mind struggling with anxiety, craziness and shadows. If there has been no

A mother accepts her child before she knows who that child will be.

- Margaret Mead and Ken Hyman

*Children grow toward
their fathers.*

**- Margaret Mead
and Ken Hyman**

*Blessed are those
who walk
in the light
of the wisdom
of joy.*

**- Torkom
Saraydarian**

blessing, the mind may live in the control of darkness.

If you are busy and in a rush, this may be the time when you place your child in front of the television. He will look with total acceptance into that technology and receive its messages and teachings.[33] In time we develop from autonomy to interdependence. From birth to age six or seven the child is totally dependent on the parents and community for not only physical nourishment but also protection and safety. From age seven to puberty the child needs to learn from trustworthy teachers to be able and safe in the world. At puberty with the changes in the pituitary gland, they become adults without experience, in need of friends and guides but less subject to control. They learn autonomy and interdependence or defensiveness and resistance.

The progression from the safety of provision and protection to trusting a teacher and growing in independence and interdependence is aided by confidence and clarity but obstructed by inappropriate confusion. Thoughts and emotions of fear and anger may be normal or they may cloud the mind and obscure our radiance as we grow. Often these are not the valid fears of actual danger to our physical safety, but illusions, projections and shame. But they can smother a young and growing purpose. The potential to uncover our light remains. Ideally, we are guided in our training, so that we know how to focus and retain the brilliance of the mind's natural potential. We can learn to guide the nervous system toward health and a meaningful way of life.

Most children are spontaneously generous with their love and their possessions. They naturally give and experience joy. However, we also see even these children learn competition and sibling rivalry. Some youngsters are cursed, wounded, or injured. They too go forth. Most of us are a mixtures of these experiences. Eventually a dominant pattern will begin to establish itself one way or the other. Life and the beauty of health can radiate from the most physically broken and crippled, while distress and dysfunction may encumber those who appear physically whole and functional. What is the critical factor? Inside each of us is a healing, self-righting capacity, a homeostasis. When body, mind, emotions, and essence maintain a balanced whole, agreement flows from us despite our flaws and is manifested in our beingness and function. Our homeostasis not only repairs physical and emotional wounds to knit our broken bones but also mends our troubled minds and maintains a connection with our soul. This unseen power of healing is part of the gift we are blessed with when we are born, part of the dynamic, unified field of nature that flows through the universe.

That which is used developes. That which is not used wastes away.

- Hippocrates

As a youth I believed the way to health was to study medicine, partly because Dr. MacDonald radiated such a joyful purpose in his work. Because it was an experience of blessing to be with him and because he worked out of his soul, I was certain that doctors knew the path to health. Years of intense study followed. In my first year of medical school, I learned of anatomy and physiology and the processes of disease. My mistakes were corrected, and I continually strove for perfection on the examinations and in laboratory experiments. Further years of study in medicine, surgery, and pharmacology prepared me for the clinical treatment of patients. I searched for the correct diagnoses, the proper medication and dosage, and came to understand health as the absence of disease or any flaws. But no one ever taught me what Dr.

My many fingers stretch to all directions your eye can see, but I point at only one thing. Who am I?

- Hippocrates

*In the center is a
seed, my soul,
planted in this body,
to be nourished in
health...*

- Gretchen Bering

MacDonald knew. No one ever taught me to work with my soul or the joy of blessing my patients. As a result, until I recovered my soul there was an absence of joy in my life and caring for people.

Our medical system is dominated by a paradigm of pathology, which invites us to rely on others to fix our defects. While we welcome and celebrate the victories of medical care over disease and illness, the medical model actually comprises only a portion of the wholeness of health. Its contribution is important but incomplete. Taken alone, the medical model may analyze inadequacies and defects, but fail to synthesize a sense of coherence and model of cooperative function in the face of change in ourselves and our environment. For those courageous enough to accept their weaknesses and go beyond, there is a trail that climbs upward to a new perspective on health.

It is a challenge to find the gifts and talents that reside in the spiritual center of our being. But the grandeur of purpose can shine so brightly that the aging process and imperfections which have blocked our creative contributions begin to shrink in significance and no longer need be formidable barriers and obstacles. When we claim our assets and resiliency it becomes possible to make an alliance with our weaknesses and come to a healthier relationship with our own essence and with other beings. All of this calls for a posture and way of life on the earth that evokes balance, no simple task in today's world. In 1975, when he saw this need to evoke balance, Jonas Salk began to advocate schools of health in addition to schools of medicine.[34]

Choosing a Conscious Life

In reality all of us are born with flaws, imperfections,

and weaknesses. If you are old enough to read this book you have been both injured and wounded. Yet you continue to stand because of the strength and integrity of the wholeness within you and around you. A sustaining harmony cycles through your vessels, throughout your body, and continually attempts to bring you back to health.

This living flow also surrounds each of us, surging through the earth and the plant and animal kingdoms, down the mountains, through the valleys and out into the sea. We honor the gift of life when we choose to be active and balanced participants in this creation of which we are a part. We honor the gift when we are conscious caretakers of ourselves and the whole. We are not irrelevant or passive observers. Receiving the gift of life is an ongoing, conscious act. We are here for a purpose.

Everything in nature has a function and participates in a continuous exchange of giving and taking. The desire of the creator, manifested in nature, seeks also to be manifest in your life. However, the universe is a permissive one. You have free will and can ignore the gift of life, the call to participate. It is easy to become distracted and diverted by the glittering lights, and forget why I am here. I can make endless choices that satisfy my pleasures, wants, and wishes, but these choices may distract me from finding wholeness and health. If I honor my gift, the information I gather will combine with my experiences of life into knowledge and wisdom. This growth is progressive, building from one event and insight to the next. It is aided or impeded by acquaintances, family, and teachers. Robert Bly, for example, attributes both the absence of purpose and senseless violence among some young urban men to their lack of older male mentors; with-

Life is what happens to us while we are making other plans unless we have learned to direct our resources toward a continuously significant future.

- Page Bailey

out such mentors young men have no connections to discernment and wisdom. No one believes in them.[35]

Bly believes this change occurred when fathers left their farms to work in factories and the sons no longer grew up working shoulder to shoulder with their fathers in the fields. Few men work on farms aided by their sons today, but some men have been able to walk with their boys into manhood. For most of us the separation and inability to be the fathers and teachers we desire is a wound carried by both sons and fathers. We are now seeing how the same change has occurred for daughters who gain their early information in day care while their mothers work. Violence from and between women is now emerging. The loss of influence of elders, is a loss not just of knowledge and information but of the discernment and wisdom that change the way a person values life itself.[36]

We learn to calculate relationships in two ways. When we make quantitative evaluations of relationships, we measure matter and energy. When we make qualitative evaluations of relationships, we measure with our mind, emotions, and soul. These different ways of measuring reflect different ways of living. In this permissive universe,[37] where we have free will, we can act and work unconscious of our purpose. We have the potential to measure only quantitatively and take more from an individual or the whole than we need or take that which belongs to another—something we would not do if we also measured qualitatively with all of our being and understood our place in the whole. Taking is balanced by giving. When we take a job as a computer programmer that we have been praying for and do nothing or give nothing in return as service to our community, we disrupt the flow. With not using our skills or talents in thanksgiving for this opportu-

Not seeing your father when you are small, never being with him, having a remote father, a workaholic father, is an injury.

- Robert Bly

In our inner cities we see gangs of fatherless youths attempting to iniate one another with no older men in sight.

- David Whyte

nity, we have taken and not returned. We have broken the cycle of reciprocity and rhythm of nature, the cycle of taking and giving.

We can become caught in a self-centered or self-serving whirlpool and hooked into a cycle of greed without realizing it. This condition will create an internal conflict and imbalance that adversely affects our health. Such people may experience symptoms of chronic anxiety, headaches that don't seem to have a reason, digestive disorders such as heart burn or chronic diarrhea, rapid breathing and numbness of the hands with tingling or even rapid heart rates and cardiac arrhythmias. One example, of giving back to the whole is the person who used his skills in computer programming as a gift of service to the Roaring Fork Outdoor Volunteers, Red Cross, local recycling center, Arbor Day Foundation, and Audubon Society. All would benefit from such talents volunteered. Even the Aspen Ski Co, CEO, has recognized this cycle as he pledged dollars for environmental programs, acknowledging "the ski industry tends to take from the environment and doesn't always give back."[38]

This is a day when life and the world seem to be standing still - only time and the river flowing past the mesas. I cannot work. I go out into the sunshine to sit receptively for what there is in this stillness and calm.

- Edith Warner

Some people, who live in abundance never come to understand the difference between the quantitative and qualitative ways of assessing life. They see not the whole, but live in scarcity with fearful eyes and are buffeted about by the rising and falling tides of ego, changing opinion, and market reports. Most of us, however, learn from family, friends, and the culture to make evaluations with our minds and souls, at least some of the time. If we are fortunate enough to be among wise elders, they will share with us an awareness of how much is enough and the subtle choices and differences that they have learned. Their language and knowledge is spiritual. It may never be measured by scientists but is the basis of their decisions in life and a means of finding purpose and calling. Spiritual wisdom is transmitted to us in the oldest stories of our species. These are stories where intention comes into meaningful alignment with purpose. Wisdom is fundamental to finding the roots of health.

Needs and Wants

Spiritual wisdom can help us to see the important subtle distinction between needs and wants. There are many things I would like, but they are not all necessary. "Necessary" is the key word that helps me distinguish between needs and wants. Most of my wants are not necessary. Not every want is a need. A need is something I must have to survive. A need is essential and without it I will experience harm. Discernment is important. I may confuse wants and needs and must be able to identify true needs from my fantasy needs. I can become addicted to fantasy needs, which will make me vulnerable to being manipulated into purchasing unnecessary things. Wants have an energy of seduction, guilt, or shame associated with them. Emotional blackmail can be used by unscrupulous people to make me vulnerable to confusing wants and needs. Awareness of what I need can help me avoid hurting myself in the pursuit of unnecessary wants.

The world has enough for everyone's need but not for everyone's greed.

- Mahatma Ghandi

Human and Natural Cycles

Activity and rest characterize all living creatures in nature. A well-conditioned man or woman can walk great distances, but will eventually become fatigued. The cycle of activity will be followed by a desire and need to stop, rest, and renew. This is the way of living systems, movement followed by recovery. We need equal amounts of each. Machinery and technology may need maintenance, but no rest. We do, and most of us get insufficient quiet and sleep. For example, in the media and the marketing of modern commerce we can lose organic time and the rhythms of quiet and recovery. To have shopping available around the clock, exceeds our human capacity. The twenty-four-hour supermarket or TV programming are too accessible for many to resist spending time and money at any moment they wish.

Time is moving faster. "The world is getting better and better and worse and worse, faster and faster."[39] The Hopi observe "time seems to be moving faster in Hopi land and elsewhere. Sometimes we feel that we are keeping up with it, then sometimes we are not."[40]

When we look at the world around us we see natural systems and movements—the rhythms of day and night, the four seasons, the rise and fall of the ocean tides. The whole of the universe dances in a natural coordinated harmony. Many cycles are so dependable and predictable that patterns of human behavior and traditions have grown to move with them. For example, the adrenal hormone secretions of our endocrine system follow a twenty-four-hour cycle called a circadian rhythm, which is dependent upon our exposure to sunlight. Our well-being requires this harmonic relationship. We become particularly aware of this requirement when we experience jet lag. This out-of-sorts feeling after long plane trips results from the way our neuroendocrine body rhythm is disturbed when travel changes our position on the earth in relationship to the sunrise. It may take us several days to reestablish this rhythm. This disturbance takes the

Experience has taught me this; that we undo ourselves with impatience

- Michel De Montaigne

A dollar is not value, but representative of value, and, at last, of moral values.

- Ralph Waldo Emerson

form of time shifts in hormone secretion, changes of body temperature and heart rate, and degradation of performance.[41]

We have inner rhythms that are always running. For nearly two thousand years it has been known that a heart removed from a body will continue to beat. Less often appreciated, however, is the fact that if this heart is kept in a perfusion solution it will maintain a circadian rhythm in relation to the sunrise.[42] Today our technology can outrun even such persistent rhythms. The shift in our heart's rhythm as a result of a plane flight to Europe may not be directly perceptible to most of us. Nevertheless, we know something isn't right for a day or two. Even with a day in an automobile the power, noise, and vibration over time will distract us. The task of driving vehicles can mesmerize us to the point that we fail to recognize fatigue and the increasing risk of making judgment errors. The same thing happens to pilots. Confidential NASA aviation safety reports state that 21 percent of "incidents" are fatigue related.[43]

The corporation, in calling for a little more creative fire from their people, must make room for a little more soul.

- David Whyte

The harmful effects of disruptive movement and work schedules are not new. In fact, the physical and emotional reactions of the early European settlers in this country to extensive traveling are stated in the Declaration of Independence. The founders of the United States were sufficiently aggravated with the King of England that they cited one of their grievances to be: "He has called together legislative bodies at places unusual, uncomfortable, and distant . . . for the sole purpose of fatiguing [the Americans]." Our founding fathers knew the need for balance between activity and rest. They recognized the need for a healthy pace of life.[44] Today, urban dwellers, seldom enjoy the pastoral life known to early Americans and the benefits of traveling on the earth by foot. Rarely do we experience a healthy sense of community associated with our movement.

Money is now the measure of what is most valued in America. The dominant view is quantitative. More is better. Time is money. Time is a commodity, one that some may consider too valuable to waste on watching sunsets. This will separate us from the natural whole and the cycle of day and night, resulting in confusion and conflicts within the natural hormonal cycles of the body. When we think of time as the equivalent to golden coins tumbling through our fingers, we have lost our sense of organic time. Organic time is the movement of day and night, summer and winter. For traditional peoples, specific times of the day and year are especially sacred such as, dawn and dusk, the equinoxes and solstices.[45] Now, however, even our most sacred days—Christmas in particular—have become times of commercial frenzy. Some cultures move slowly enough to hold sacred values higher than money. They respect natural rhythms and the need for a day of rest each week to balance work and creating wealth.[46]

While seeming to have less time now, we have also lost a sense of the sacred. We have the technology to outrun the cycle of work and rest. Money, our most potent symbol and measure of power, now never rests. When there is no rest for the dollars we value most, then our own exhaustion and fatigue become risks to our health. An increased life span may not mean that we live longer and have more choices but that although we move faster we die longer.[47] Is that our intention? The clock provides a technical measurement of how long we live. Far more real than time ticking away on the clock is the way we open up the

The money which a man possesses is the instrument of freedom; that which we eagerly pursue is the instrument of slavery.

- Jean-Jacques Rousseau

Money is like muck, not good except it be spread.

- Francis Bacon

minutes and hours and invest them with meaning. Death is not the greatest tragedy in life. The ultimate tragedy is to die without discovering the possibilities of our full growth.[48]

The Rhythm of the Earth

The cumulative effects from decades of jet lag among military and commercial flight crews and travelers may not be known for years to come. But I observe the effects of modern life and travel on heart rate and blood pressure. Among my patients, I discern differences between people who calmly work outside in one place and people who are constantly busy in traffic as delivery people, truck or bus drivers. I particularly remember the day John, a Native American, came to me as a patient. He had been injured in an automobile accident. He was no longer able to work. He was also depressed and discouraged because he had lost his home and car. However, when I listened to his blood pressure I experienced something that had never happened before in my thirty years of taking this vital sign. Despite his situation, the sound and movement of blood in John's body came to me as if I were listening to the pulse of the earth. His heart rate and blood pressure rose slow and strong, and the readings were much lower than normal.

I was transfixed; this was a man of the land different from the farmers and ranchers I had cared for across the United States. Even with an injury his being and blood flowed with the rhythm of the earth, slow and steady.

Schweitzer's heart began to move with the rhythm of the earth, in Africa. At the edge of the primeval

Without silence we become frightened by what is occuring. There is no room for it to grow inside us, and bereft of that spaciousness, we feel as if the process is about to take us over.

- David Whyte

African forest he began to experience a change away from the civilization of Europe. Such a relationship with the earth is unfamiliar to most urban dwellers. We are no longer a civilization that listens to the earth and nature. Although the rhythmic pulse of the natural symphony continues, the dominant culture has tuned its ear and pace to the hum of engines and unrelenting tempo of technology. Over the years the rhythm of the earth has become more distant as traffic and technology have progressed.

Schweitzer considered striving for material progress to be characteristic of modern Europeans and people of European descent. He believed this grew out of their world outlook. "Enthusiasm for progress has taken possession of" the modern European and American. "It is upon this will to material progress, acting in conjunction with the will to ethical progress, that modern civilization is founded."[49] Surrounded by nature Schweitzer struggled with the philosophical relationship between material and ethical progress. It troubled him.

Eighty years ago he could see the bond with ethics "loosening and finally breaking apart" and "will end in disintegration. . . . Humanity is being guided by a will to progress that has become merely external and has lost its bearings. . . . Only if it turns inward and becomes ethical can the will to progress attain the ability to distinguish the valuable from the worthless. We must therefore strive for a civilization that is not based on the accretion of science and power alone, but which cares most of all for the spiritual and ethical development of the individual and humankind."[50]

It was at this time on a jungle river and among people whose tradition was primitive and moving with the

Talking Health but Doing Sickness.

**- Patricia Kinloch
Health Services
Researcher in Samoa**

cycles of nature, that his guiding philosophy of "reverence for life" was born. It came out of his relationship with the African earth. There are two references which provide understanding about the setting in which this concept revealed itself to Schweitzer. In the first reference he wrote that while he was struggling with this dilemma in the summer of 1915, "I was wandering about in a thicket where no path was to be found." In this mental state he had to take a long journey up the Ogowe River for 160 miles. Slowly he traveled upstream lost in thought sitting on the deck of a barge. On the third day at sunset as they were making their way through a herd of hippopotamuses there flashed upon Schweitzer's "mind, unforeseen and unsought, the phrase "reverence for life."[51]

In a changing world each individual must change and find a place for himself.

- Albert Schweitzer

In a second reference Schweitzer recalled for Norman Cousins that it was while he was in Africa gliding up the Ogowe many years ago—passing one of the luxuriant islands in the river and looking up at the scudding clouds that the idea of "reverence for life came to him."[52]

Each springtime I take time to paddle my kayak on a river alone immersed in the nourishment of nature. Something happens to me there away from civilization in the desert wilderness that nourishes my soul. My emotions and essence catch up with me as I paddle. All of me comes together. While I am at work I give attention to the continuous reports of my mind and body. My brain is bursting and my bottom is tired of sitting. But to hear my emotions and essence, I need to create conditions which allow them to get through to me. I set aside time so they can be heard. A calm walk also allows me to gather not only my thoughts, but also my ignored and scattered emotions and essence. My walk has now become a pilgrimage for I regularly invite my soul to travel along.

Walking

As we walk we naturally come to respect the balance between activity and rest. This respect will allow us to continue walking for many years. We may acquire some blisters if we are not conditioned or do not properly care for our feet, but rarely do we sustain a serious injury. Postal workers who walk as mail carriers have fewer complaints of low back pain than those who stand or sit in the post office building. Women who walk ten miles per day as meter readers have far fewer degenerative discs in their lower backs than women who sit at computer terminals in an office all day.[53]

Truck drivers have more herniated discs in their low backs than any other workers. Moreover, natural movement has a different effect on our presence and overall health than technology. Natural movement is by foot. As children we run and play, but as we mature, our pace settles to a walk. Traveling on our feet at a comfortable pace tones our heart, strengthens our bones and muscles, and soothes the emotions, mind, and soul. We can travel alone or with a companion; in contemplation, as well as in conversation. However, traveling by foot confines us to a small geographic area and, by modern standards, limits our choices and opportunities.

The once familiar activity of an early morning walk, which served the purpose of getting us somewhere while allowing us to greet and speak with our neighbors, is now infrequent. A walk in the woods is rare. However, a curious variation of this activity has developed in athletic clubs and homes. People now walk on treadmills for exercise. Although going nowhere purposeful, they walk to benefit their heart muscle. Of

A man ought to have a doctor's prescription to be allowed to use a golf cart.

- Paul Dudley White

Walk as children of light.

- Ephesians 5:8

course, walking on a treadmill does strengthen the cardiovascular system, but it does not nourish the mind and soul as would a positive interaction with friends and community. It does not renew our wholeness the way a walk in nature will.

Artist Julia Cameron advocates walking twenty minutes daily and one hour per week for creativity. She writes, "Walking is the most powerful creative tool that I know. Although it has fallen into disuse in our hurried times, it may be the most powerful spiritual practice known to man."[54] "Walking opens us up." It sustains us as we do the work necessary to shape and reshape our lives. She has a wonderful phrase: "walking with our soles is really walking with our souls."[55] Inviting our souls to be with us as we walk can be healing. "A vigorous five-mile walk will do more good for an unhappy but otherwise healthy adult than all of the medicine and psychology in the world."[56]

This kind of discourse is considered "soft data" by the objective standards of medical research. I was taught to respect that which I could see and that which has been proven by scientific testing. I was discouraged from experiencing and feeling emotions, and since my essence could not be found under the microscope, both of these parts of myself were neglected. But they inevitably showed up when I began to ambulate. Taking a quiet walk will frequently bring up for me, feelings I have been overlooking and neglecting. It is no longer healthy for me to run away from my fear, grief, or anger. My soul receives the renewing energy of the earth as I walk. I am not whole without my soul.

Emotions are normal and flow through me as the river flows down the valley. Emotions are life energy

Your vision will become clear only when you can look into your own heart. Who looks outside, dreams; who looks inside, awakes.

- Carl Jung

moving through my being, though no one ever described it that way to me in my medical training. Rather, my medical education cautioned me about the hazards of emotions, it was said they were irrational. The soul was ignored even more; it was never mentioned. I was taught by its absence not to acknowledge it. I was not encouraged to bring it in the door of the hospital, and my medical associates for the most part have not wanted it in the office, either. These two aspects of me are always getting lost, and I am continuously getting myself together. Taking a walk in the woods or beside the still waters restores my soul. My essence is nourished in nature. The simple act of walking allows me to receive and integrate information from all of my parts: mind, body, emotions, and essence. Walking recharges and renews. The beauty of walking is that the whole body benefits. As emotions surface, I experience them, and often a creative insight transforms the meaning of the event. *Solvitur ambulando*: it is solved by walking, said Saint Augustine.

When I trust my feelings, I am usually right.

- Anne Wilson Schaef

Emotions and Essence

Emotions were ignored as I grew up. The culture reinforced this. Medicine puts little emphasis on feelings. When feelings such as depression, pain, or sadness arise, medications are quickly prescribed to dull these experiences. "We are deluged with facts, but we have lost or are losing, our human ability to feel them."[57] Although we infrequently acknowledge emotions, a relationship is emerging in the dissatisfaction we have with trying to find meaning in our work. For better or worse the unity of mind, matter, and meaning is intact and functioning in our bodies every day. Meaning is always physically active.[58] "Meaning is

Despite having learned the power of that which is not readily visible, physicians as a profession have not caught up altogether with other powerful non-visible toxic agents, namely, feelings.

- Harry Levinson

being."[59] and people who are dissatisfied with their work manifest physical symptoms and disease. "Meaning is inseparable from . . . thoughts, feelings, and emotions . . . meaning and emotion are on a continuum."[60] Job dissatisfaction links meaning and emotions with Monday morning heart attacks and low back disability[61]. Emotions are part of the meaning of life which flows through us. They are not rational, and are not supposed to be. Emotions and meaning are unique to each person, but some generalizations about feelings and their functions are useful.

There are five root emotions: grief, fear, anger, love and joy. We experience each of these feelings for a specific reason. In grief I release both energy and emotion. Grief makes me tired, but if I don't let it go, I feel even more drained. Grief becomes heavy. Releasing it creates space as I empty out. Grief is a natural help in releasing. With this physical discomfort, I cry. It feels like my guts are being torn out. That happens when I am trying to hold on. I hold on because of fear, it is physically uncomfortable to release and let go. But in order to grieve I must let go and release. The process of grief teaches me this.

Fear is a natural physical motivator. It calls on me to move out of the way of danger. To freeze in fear is a learned response or a conflict of emotions, in either case, a shut down of all systems. Because fear is a physical body motivator, it has the ability to send information to the entire body. Fear says be aware and is meant to get my adrenal glands going, so that I am not in a stupor. Fear can also be used to maneuver and manipulate people. Politicians can use fear to control people.

Anger cleanses my emotional state. When my ideas

It is extremely difficult to grasp the idea that feelings are the primary participants of behavior and a major influence in health and sickness.

- Harry Levinson

You can't change a feeling state without changing the cognitive process that produces it.

- Page Bailey

and plans are blocked and obstructed, I become frustrated and angry. The energy of anger can help mobilize me to get through the blockages. I develop new ideas and make new plans. When I acknowledge and know what the natural purpose of the emotion is, I am less vulnerable to being in conflict or confusion. Not knowing that anger is to cleanse me will interfere with my ability to make more appropriate decisions.

Love is the energy of creativity. The energy of creating children, art, dance and music. It naturally motivates me to move into creativity. When I am unable to manifest my creation I get angry. Anger is available to help push me through the block of not being creative.

Joy is the basic natural recharge and rejuvenation. It makes me feel good, calm, and elated as a part of the whole. Joy is naturally related to love and helps me keep balanced, so that I do not become bogged down in grief, fear, or anger. When a person communicates with his essence, he feels the joy existing in the human heart.[62] We have much joy in our natures, but we do not enjoy it because we are in too much of a hurry. An active flow of joy is a cause of health, happiness, energy, optimism and enthusiasm.[63] When you experience joy, try to sustain it for several hours. One minute of joy can make you a healthier person for months. When people are in a hurry they eat like dogs. They do not chew their food, but swallow it very fast. If they would take the time to chew their food, they would enjoy tasting the food. They would have the opportunity to assimilate the food and use it for their well being. This is true for everything we want to enjoy. Do not hurry. The moment of joy is a sacred moment of transformation.[64]

Being aware of feelings is essential to being whole and

The magnet of materialism is keeping people too busy to hear about spiritual change.

- Somé

As joy increases, the purpose of life appears more and more clearly.....

- Torkom Saraydarian

receiving the teaching of the emotions. Emotions do not necessarily make sense. For example, in nature and great music or art, emotions are evoked which we may not understand. "There is a road from the eye to the heart that does not go through the intellect."[65] Something powerful, but unexplainable wells up inside of me. Being with an emotion is not a static process. The emotion moves like a river, it flows through me and travels on. It is when emotions become stuck that problems more often occur.

These are the root emotions from which all others manifest as combinations. But in today's information-mechanical-technical world feelings and meaning are discounted.[66] "For science, meaning does not exist."[67] "We are all more or less in danger of becoming human things instead of personalities."[68] said Schweitzer as he saw the consequences of losing confidence in ourselves and our thinking. We have become lost "in the nonessential."[69] Emotions are as much a part of us as our arms and legs. Together with the essence, they register meaning. Pay attention to your feelings and trust that they are for your protection. Awareness can help us from hurting ourselves.

Some people also call awe or mystery an emotion and this is where the relationship between feelings and the essence can be seen most clearly. Einstein said, "The most beautiful and most profound emotion we can experience is the sensation of the mystical. It is the sower of all true science. He to whom this emotion is stranger, who can no longer wonder and stand rapt in awe, is as good as dead."[70]

For the more one discovers of God, the more one finds one has to learn.

- Bede Griffiths

Being in the emotion of awe, in a state of mystery, is a dynamic state of union with the creative flow of the universe. The essence is our bridge and connection to mystery. Allowing the space and time to be filled with awe and mystery, when they are present to us, is being in relationship with wholeness. Being in awe is not simply emotional or physical or mental; mystery, most certainly, involves our soul. All of us stand in a humble state of wonder. To receive the fullness of that experience, requires the wisdom not to reach for another bite of food, when I am already enjoying the tasty morsel in my mouth.

Inability to recognize an emotional gift can result in my running from one experience to another without fully owning the abundance of being where I am.

*When you do wake,
you are rousing a
different part of you,
a barely experienced
life that lies
at your core.*

- David Whyte

> I am not thinking about going
> Nor collecting myself from coming
>
> I am simply here—whole on the
> Earth with my Creator
>
> I am not down in the valley where I look
> But up on the ridge in the wind
>
> I have found my essence—here
> Where I have been all the time

*The moment of
harmony will always
be the Present Moment,
between balance
and imbalance.*

- Rob Baker

The Training of a Physician

I did not know any of this as a young physician. I did not truly know about life as a gift, about cycles in nature or about the meaning of emotions. Sometimes I was blessed, but not always; I did not understand that either. I had obtained the knowledge and confidence that comes with the intensity of a modern med-

*He sings to me and
calls my name from
somewhere up there
Over there, from
somewhere here, from
the depths of our minds.*

**- Yup'ik Eskimo
Song**

*Every plank of science's
advance is first laid ....
by the spontaneous
conjectures of
instinctive reason.*

- Charles S. Pierce

ical education. Hours of lectures by professors knowl-edgeable in the physiology and pathology of their specialties impressed me with their depth of understanding. They answered all questions with confidence and covered all possible conditions. There seemed to be a solution for every human problem. It was simply a matter of time and dedication until the scientific method in which I was trained would methodically plow up the final vestiges of disease and suffering. And it is true that I have seen many miracles in medicine in my lifetime.

The fear of children crippled by the plague of polio haunted my mother, but the anxiety permeating swimming pools and beaches was lifted away by the Salk and Sabin vaccines. Salk himself said, "What had the most profound effect was the freedom from fear." Medical marvels have multiplied. Even the human heart and vessels are surgically entered, repaired, and transplanted. My confidence took on an arrogance that blinded me to the deeper meaning of health and to the wisdom of traditional practitioners for many years. I cured pneumonia with antibiotics, relieved heart failure with cardiac stimulants and diuretics, delivered babies, repaired wounds, and casted fractures. I was a part of a medical team that could do wonders and save lives.

But beneath my confidence were feelings I did not understand. Early in my medical career in Alaska talking over great distances on the radio telephone from remote islands to close friends, fellow physicians or with patients or village medical aids I would sometimes be puzzled by the emotions which I experienced. My reaction was embarrassment, a feeling I would quickly shut down, because to even have such an experience suggested a flaw in my masculinity and scientific training.

When I flew into the remote Alaskan village of Nondalton as a young doctor to hold a clinic, it did not occur to me to ask any questions of Harry Nicolai, the traditional healer of the village. My emotions and essence were shut down. Modern medicine and technology would defeat disease and death, and I knew about all of these things. What I did not recognize was how little I knew about the soul, healing, and nature. I did not recognize that these people survived through a perception that I would not come to understand or value until decades later.

Many thousands of years of human knowledge and tools have accumulated to create a storeroom of technological implements and medications upon which I can draw and around which my activities revolve. Over the past eighty years we have dramatically increased our physical and mental capacities with inventions. In many cases these inventions have come to dominate our attention, our lives, and the planet.

All choices effect my health in either positive or negative ways.

- Page Bailey

Choice

The ethics and values we use as a basis for guiding our power and organizing our lives and culture must work functionally for the whole, economically and spiritually for young and old, men and women. They should come from our accumulated wisdom and ability to discern inner qualities and relationships. Today, our values and technology are on a collision course. This became clear to me one day in a hospital emergency department. A woman had died in the hospital early in the morning. Her elderly husband, Ed Miller, had been with her during her passing, and as a volunteer was walking with him down the hallway afterward, Ed experienced a cardiac arrest. Within moments, he was in the emergency room, where I successfully defibrillated him and admitted him to the coronary care unit. Many resuscitations are unsuccessful, and I was feeling good about my morning work until I talked with Ed Miller later in the afternoon. He told me, "I am eighty-seven years old and have finished my time on this earth—I no longer wish to live." Upon hearing this I had to reevaluate my actions and whether I had used my training and tools appropriately.

Because there was no significant damage evident to Ed Miller's heart, he was discharged quickly despite his age. Only a few days later, his son brought him back. He had experienced another cardiac arrest in the car. This time I talked with his son at the front of the hospital. I did not act. We both knew that his father had no desire to prolong his life, even though I had the technology to try.

To save a man's life against his will is the same as killing him.

- Horace

A crack had developed in the shell of certainty I had constructed around doing my medical practice. I had learned with my brain the importance of matching the proper treatment to the patient's physical needs. But my focus was on the patient's body and my own desire to perform technological procedures flawlessly, as I had been trained to do. I had the power to restart a heart and lengthen the life of a man's physical vessel. But that had not been Ed Miller's goal. His mind, emotions, and essence had reached an agreement with his body to leave this world. My training had taught me that when I restarted a heart, *my* heart could not be involved. I could not allow it to be. Emotions might interfere with clear judgment. In my training, death was failure, and physicians did not contemplate death or failure. No one had prepared me to be a guide over the bridge from life to death.

Instead, I had been trained to act with a speed that could ignore the value of honoring Ed Miller's place in the whole and his desire to pass from life to death. Once the certainty of Ed's readiness to make that passage stood stark before me, I placed that choice first.

A spiritual value began to influence my *being* and it imbued my medical and scientific *doing*. Spiritual progress calls for a re-evaluation of the physical world, whether care of the physical body or attachment to material possessions. The speed with which each generation must make value-based decisions is accelerating. The potential health consequences of actions by an individual, a government, or a multinational corporation can be enormous. For example, only in recent years has the cumulative effect of burning fossil fuels been recognized as the "greenhouse effect" of warming the earth's atmosphere. The United States and the industrialized world produce the majority of the heat-trapping gases in the atmosphere. The growing "ozone hole" is another atmospheric consequence of collective human technical progress and activity. Chloroflurocarbons and their chemical relatives deplete the ozone layer.

Information is expanding, but the wisdom of past generations is being lost and, with it, knowledge that affects our values—wisdom of the sacredness of life. This wisdom is not heard or acted upon unless we intend for our ears to listen and our hearts to receive.

Our ancestors' wisdom is still valid, but more difficult for us to see as we are watching the very foundation of our lives change. When I worked in the garden with my father I learned the long-handled shovel could be used to spade the earth or dig a hole. He taught me to clean the mud off the blade before I put the shovel

If work is about doing, then the soul is all about being; *The indiscriminate enjoyer of everything that comes our way. If work is the world, the soul is the home.*

- David Whyte

For whatever the source of masculine abuse of power, it is our responsibility as contemporary men to understand it and to develop the emotional and spiritual resources to end it.

- Robert Moore and Douglas Gillette

away, so rust would not form in the metal. The blade would hold an edge longer, and with care the shovel could be useful for many years. Today we seldom use our parents' and grandparents' tools or the knowledge and methods that went with them; new knowledge and technology have overgrown the past. The result is that we are pulled in two directions, between a heritage that sometimes doesn't seem to fit and future that we don't understand.

For example, we and our children are learning to use computers, the basic components of the information-mechano-technological age. With these new tools we can write a letter, speed communication, run a corporation, or fight a war. Computers serve individuals, companies, governments, and the military. Simultaneously, we pass to our children the value systems that guide the use of such equipment. Value systems that, too often, are no longer grounded in nature or reverence for life. Without clear intention we can become confused with this information overload. The mind seeks and wants stimulation. It must be guided in constructive behavior and requested to move in a healthy direction.[71] Or it will pass countless hours seeking the stimulation of the internet, TV, or video games. Hours that turn into days, weeks, months and years—a lifetime of meaningless stimulation. A lifetime without an authentic purpose.

*The road to the
sacred leads through
the secular.*

- Abraham Heschel

"Meaninglessness is equivalent to illness, because it inhibits fullness in life."[72] Fullness leads to wholeness and balance. The intellect is creative, yet not as powerful as the heart and feelings. The intellectual man will prove unbalanced in the end if he has no feeling side to his being.[73]

Today we are challenged as never before to integrate

the old with the new, spiritual values with technological advances, and meaning with intellect if we are to retain our connection to the whole, our health and our purpose. We cannot pass a well-synthesized set of values to our offspring until we achieve the synthesis of these values for ourselves.

Seventy years ago Schweitzer observed, "All progress in discovery and invention evolves at last to a fatal result, if we do not maintain control over it through a corresponding progress in our spirituality."[74] The first step on the path to spiritual progress is to acknowledge the essence, the soul, and receive the gift of its teaching and mystery. With that perspective, "man does not simply accept his existence as something given, but experiences it as something unfathomably mysterious."[75] In America, "the soul—that deep, hidden, knowing sense within—is malnourished. We mistakenly thought that the intellect was the avenue to experiencing the sacred, to nourishing the soul. We discounted the imagination and other faculties essential to knowing mystery."[76]

The messages to the soul are subtle. Schweitzer summarized Goethe's philosophy in these words, "In a whisper God speaks in our heart; very low and very clear he lets us know what is to be chosen and what is to be shunned."[77] Constant awareness is necessary to hear the whisper. "The alteration between rigor and gentleness, between rational process and mystery, between activity and the absence of activity does not permit an alteration between awareness and a lack of awareness. The alteration between rigor and gentleness is a choice that is made at a high level of awareness."[7] The challenge to be aware and mindful comes from all ancient traditions and teachers. This teaching is available from the authentic elders of our own and other cultures.

Where is the wisdom we have lost in knowledge?
Where is the knowledge we have lost in information?

- T.S. Eliot

.. you have purpose, because you have soul.

- Torkom Saraydarian

We of the Kennedy and Johnson administration who participated in the decisions on Vietnam acted according to what we thought were the principles and traditions of this nation. We made our decisions in light of those values.

- Robert McNamara

Or we can also naively believe we are getting the best from our new tools by supporting technological idealism, but the hidden price tag of this illusion is corporate profit at the expense of human health.[79] Technology is the fruit of human creativity but it requires conscious human guidance. Unless technology is used altruistically, it is at risk of becoming a tool of human frailty and greed. Altruism is that which is best for all concerned including yourself. If we lose the values that worked for our ancestors, as well as traditional peoples, if we abandon values, such as altruism without understanding them, we loose our roots in the earth and health. Altruism calls for the reciprocity of give and take. Yet for such values to work they must come alive in us. Man will not conquer nature, for nature holds the last card. If the future is to be viable, it will be one in which humanity cooperates with nature.[80]

If we simply turn away in silence, and believe we are inadequate to this challenge, then there will be no boundaries and no values. Without the guidance of our cooperative values and wholeness progress will evolve toward a fatal result. If there is no intention to claim health and wholeness, the drift of meaningless stimulation will continue to keep us busy, but going nowhere.

A ponderosa pine has many cones upon its branches. Each cone contains many seeds. All seeds carry the potential to start the life of a new tree. Sunshine falls upon all of them equally. Some seeds fall on the granite and never take root. Other seeds become food for the blue jay and the squirrel. Only a very few seeds will grow into giant trees. There are many possibilities. We each have many possibilities. The first decision is whether to care for the gift of life with reverence.

Your attitude toward the gift will determine the relationship between your mind, body, emotions, and essence. Not all will perceive their gift to be sacred and give thanks. Not all will claim what they have been given. To claim health we must actively and consciously guide and use the gift. Schweitzer knew this when he began the root idea of his theory of the universe with "my relation to <u>my own being</u> and to the objective world is determined by reverence for life."(Emphasis added)[81] He saw that in order to have reverence for others it was first necessary to claim this for himself.

"I give my existence a meaning from within outwards."[82] When I claim respect for myself, I am able to extend respect to others and the earth. This is not easy for Americans. It is not arrogance. It is not charity. It is an act of great courage to work with the inevitable fear, which will be present once we get past the arrogance of our minds. If we don't make an alliance with this fear we will remain separated from the confidence that comes with the fullness of our gift and a meaningful purpose. This fear of receiving and containing the gift is so great that two centuries ago, Ben Franklin saw the consequence of such choices when he observed, "Nine men in ten are suicides."[83]

Cynicism will never bring us the power we need to face our planetary challenges.

- Robert Moore and Douglas Gillette

Fear of failure hinders a beginning.

- Dhyani Ywahoo

CHAPTER 3

TO BE OR NOT TO BE

Listen to the natural rhythm of your breath,
listen to the natural rhythm of your heart. This
is the key to your right to be.

Lané Saán

*... I am alone with
the beating of my
heart....*

- Lui Chi

In order for me to hear the rhythm of my heart I must
experience either great stillness or great exertion. I
was first aware of my heartbeat while climbing. As a
youth rapidly ascending above timberline my heart
would pound in my chest, I could feel that. But Lané
taught me that she learned to claim her 'right to be' by
listening to the rhythm of her heart all of the time.
This was a more subtle perception. However, she
came from a different culture and was able to listen in
ways unfamiliar to me. Ways which I had forgotten or
never knew.

*Learning to sustain
this inner quiet is
perhaps one of the
more harrowing
experiences the
human soul goes
through in its quest
for deepening.*

- David Whyte

In order to listen to my heartbeat under less than
strenuous conditions I have to become calm and still.
Immediately the hardest thing to quiet down is my
mind. It is always busy, chattering away. But when I
set aside time away from telephones, schedules, and
lists of things to do, I can eventually hear what my
heart is saying. Stillness is as important to my health
as activity. Only a limited amount of information can
enter into my mind at any one time. When I do get
quiet information can begin to register if the TV, telephone, radio, and fax machine are shut off. Then I can
receive my physical information: what I see, hear, feel,
taste, smell; my balance, hunger and pain. Mental
information: lists of things to do, ideas, solutions,
options, words, and phrases. Emotional information:

joy, love, grief, fear, and anger. Spiritual information: awe, creativity, inspiration and thanksgiving. I thank my parts for what they have shared with me. Then after all these reports have come in, stillness arrives—sometimes not quickly. But in time it arrives and I hear the voice of the Creator. The emptiness that is filled with God.

Stillness

This information arises from a safe place of quiet and calm. A place still enough for me to hear the rhythm of my heart and the healing voice. The Creator speaks to me through beauty, dreams, feelings, intuition, symbols, and waking visions.[1] There are many descriptions for this place of quiet and stillness. A calm lake without a ripple on the surface is one such image. It is called by some the "spirit lake of quietness," the house of the healer within. For most people the "spirit lake of quietness" has been invaded and consumed by their preoccupation with the material world.[2] However, when they are able to become quiet they can again begin to know the Creator. A sacred way of being, hearing and seeing develops.

A sacred view of the world is one of reverence for all of my own parts and all life around me. It comes from deep within. The nature of all our relationships changes with a perception of reverence. A sacredness of both knowledge and place live together where I stand on the earth. A desire begins to grow in me to move in a sacred manner whether I am in the market place, with family, or among friends. How I speak, how I see and how I relate are all transformed. But I do not do this alone, the light of the creator is flowing through me. My community supports or denies my sacredness.

In a state wherein the grosser mind becomes inactive, then the subtler mind becomes more active...

- The Dali Lama

It would be a distortion to imply this ideal is constant. I am always in the process of regaining my balance. Because I know this place, seeking it is my constant intention. But doubt does surface. Because we humans are innately insecure, we doubt. So continuously, a contest is going on between knowing and trusting my sacredness or shriveling in doubt and fear. The place of knowing is alive and experienced with all of my parts. It is a place of mystery. To learn to trust, I begin with trusting myself and then others. A community of trust is able to become cooperative.

A community of fear competes, but never really knows authentic cooperation and trust. To live in a place of trust is an experience that goes beyond our present understanding. Schweitzer knew that a "reverence for life leads us into a spiritual relationship with the world independent of a full understanding of the universe. . . . It is not through knowledge, but through experience of the world that we are brought into relationship with it. . . . What is rational reaches eventually the non-rational."[3]

A man who fears suffering is already suffering from what he fears.

- Michel de Montaigne

I must make an active choice everyday to respect myself. The roots of my sacredness sink deep into the earth. Knowing my sacredness, I believe and think differently than when my doubt is controlling me.
I choose to respect myself.

Respect

"Respect is the key to living."[4] Respect is the first step on the path.[5] But being respected in America today may not be a given. Individual value and respect in this culture are achieved through success in competition. This is measured by position of influence and wealth. Acknowledgment or reverence for a person's inherent value in being is eclipsed by these outward gauges of success. In fact, one of the consequences of the progress resulting from the industrial revolution and today's technological improvements has been a loss of the ability to bless and pass on sacred values. Consequently there has been a destabilization of the marriage bond and family unit. As Borysenko, Bradshaw, Dossey and others have pointed out, shame has become widespread and is toxic and disempowering. There is no respect in shame. Shame-based parents are unable to take care of a child's needs. When the child becomes an adult there is a "hole in his soul."[6] When shame-based people find and marry each other they expect their mate to take care of them and parent the unfulfilled child within them.[7]

In contrast, traditional cultures saw the sacredness of each person in their being, before they ever perform an action. Thus, respect in Native American cultures has a different orientation from contemporary America. Abraham Maslow told a relevant story about respect. He was with the Blackfoot when a child wanted out of a cabin, where he was with a group of adults. The cabin door was large and heavy; the child struggled unsuccessfully with it. Maslow said he considered getting up to open the door for the youngster, but the elders simply sat while the child worked and pushed as hard as he could. After about 30 minutes the little one did succeed in opening the door. Then the adults were up on their feet surrounding him and celebrating his achievement with praise. He was able to get it done himself. Maslow said he then realized that these people respected this child more than he did.[8]

There is an important subtlety here. The Blackfoot adults blessed the child's 'right to be' and held a

The task of the Whole Man is to help others; that's my firm teaching, that's my message.

- The Dali Lama

The quality of the action of a person who is whole differs from the quality of other's actions. What he says, the way he looks at people: the deep effect that is left is due to the fact that it comes from a different source of action, a different layer of inner being.

- Seyyed Hossein Nasr

sacred space for him while he worked to open the door. The adults did not view this as an achievement of individual selfish will, but rather an important event for the entire community as the child took a step toward claiming his 'right to be' as a responsible and useful participant in his village. Blessing a person's 'right to be' is fundamental to the Native American view of life and health. This was a daily teaching which was emphasized at the time of special ceremonies. In the Apache tradition the most important community event was the Blessingway at the time of a young girls first menses. A measure of the significance of this occurred during the 1882 flight of Geronimo and his band to Mexico, as travel was halted to celebrate a young girl's puberty (Blessingway) ceremony, while they were under pursuit by the U. S. Army.[9]

From childhood we must develop the balance between earthly and heavenly values.

- Torkom Saraydarian

The Blackfoot, like most people in history, recognize each individual as someone of special purpose with a right to be. When a community of people accept this, there is a recognition of the need also to responsibly care for the earth. Earth guardians know that we all owe to the universal order, and it is impossible at this level, to do for others what they are expected to do for themselves. We owe to the universal order because we are responsible for its maintenance.[10] We are powerful creatures, and here for a purpose. Respect for the earth is as necessary as respect for ourselves.

For God did not give us a spirit of timidity, but a spirit of power, of love and of self discipline.

- II Timothy 1:7

The 'right to be' is honored from the birth of a Native American child. The youngster learns to claim this 'right' is by listening to the rhythm of his heart. This does not even sound normal for the dominant American culture of today where attention is centered on the intellectual processes and directed toward the fulfillment and gratification of individual desires and wants. While ignoring the emotions and essence, the momentum of our culture moves in the pursuit of what the mind and body seek. The contemporary cultural message is: Go for the profit, you cannot afford to listen to your heart. Understandable though this attitude is for surviving today, it creates a difficulty if you seek the path to health. Listening to the heart is the initial step in hearing the needs and purpose of the soul.

Heart

One does not learn about the 'right to be' by reasoning with the mind alone. The heart must open. Schweitzer listened with all of his parts, including his heart when he was moved by his essence to leave behind a career as a theologian, author, and the most famous organist and interpreter of the works of Johann Sebastian Bach in Europe. Schweitzer studied medicine and established a hospital in Africa. Reason could warn him of the difficulties involved in this plan, but it required the total commitment of his mind, body, emotions, and essence to fulfill the vision.

Similarly, Sir Edmund Hillary is most often remembered as the man who first climbed Mount Everest, but his passion and vision were actually channeled into being a builder of schools and medical clinics in Nepal. We may each experience life through the needs of our mind, or our body, or our emotions, or our soul. My experience is that each of my parts want to speak and to vote. No one wants to be ignored. What works best is to integrate all of these parts cooperatively. But to process an event with my heart is very different from merely knowing the experience cognitively. A child who learns to listen to her heart will know more

..the salvation of this human world lies nowhere else than in the human heart, in the human power to reflect, in human meekness and in human responsibility.

- Vaclav Havel

The denial of the fire of truth in yourself is going to be the denial of your heart's beat --- maybe make your arteries hard or something like that.

- **Dhyani Ywahoo**

The child's growing need to take in the world soon becomes as acute as hunger or thirst.

- **Margaret Mead and Ken Hyman**

than just her cardiovascular aerobic capacity. She will also be able to access all of the feeling and wisdom available to one who follows the path of the heart. "See the beauty in your own heart."[11] This is the ancient way written in the heart of every man and woman.[12]

There are still cultures of the heart. But the dominant American culture and population is focused in the head. We are experiencing the consequences of when the combined act of feeling and thinking became replaced by thinking, alone. The machine has overturned the heart and sits in its place and is being worshipped as spiritual. "This is simply an error in human judgment. Anyone who worships his own creation, something of his own making, is someone in a state of confusion."[13] What is the price of ignoring the heart in American culture? It is impossible to calculate, but it is interesting to note that heart disease continues to remain the number one cause of death in the United States.

Many devices today make life "easier" and more convenient, while we struggle to retain our inner awareness and the rhythm of our heart. Much of this is a consequence of speed. The 'right to be' is obscured by the revolutions per minute of production schedules, the hands of the clock, miles per hour of the auto, or by information overload. The Native American had and still have very little materially, by modern standards, yet their hearts travel with them. Many of them still carry their 'right to be' and a wisdom which we have lost or never known.

Knowledge is cumulative. Different cultures developed and built different types of knowledge. Cross cultural knowledge can benefit our weaknesses. The principles and discoveries of our technological achievements and language did not erupt spontaneously out of World War II, but were built in a progressive manner over centuries. Modern information systems can now collect, copy, and distribute enormous amounts of data. Similarly, other systems of understanding have developed over centuries. Learning from other knowledge sources is optional in the permissive universe. Information is not necessarily wisdom. Honoring the right of a child to listen to the rhythm of his heart is wisdom. Ignoring this right separates the child from an important part of himself and results in young people who are insecure. Children who become filled with anger that can lead to violence or the inevitable depression of when one fails to claim a meaningful purpose.

The backbone and wisdom of the Apache and Navajo medical systems is the Blessingway ceremony.[14] Over a series of four days, a person is the center of celebration of all the powers of the universe, with family and friends. This creates a safe and blessed space, but much more than that. Inherent in "the right to be" is the concept of empowerment in alignment and harmony with the creator and all of nature. All evil is excluded from the Blessingway ceremony, and the subject and community see each other as beautiful and vital creatures. The harmony of the individual is celebrated and restored by the community. The Blackfoot did not sit while the child struggled to open the cabin door in a manner of detachment, they rather held a sacred space of blessing and empowerment for the youngster. A sacred space is virtually unknown in most of modern America. This ancient sacredness of communal respect for personal value contrasts sharply with isolated individuals in the pursuit of selfish fulfillment. Empowerment in the context of

We believe both men and women have encoded deep inside an understanding of how to use their power for blessing and liberation. With the Navajo, we have faith that human beings can once again find the "Blessingway".

- Robert Moore and Douglas Gillette

meaningful participation in a group is also different from the dependency, disability, and welfare systems of America today.

When I realized the meaning and significance of the "Blessingway," with it came the awareness that my medical education was not characterized by blessings. The joy and healing of Dr. MacDonald has faded from American medicine. To complete medical training one must be thick skinned and tough enough to take lots of correction, criticism and shaming. In order to gain the skill to competently practice today's technological medicine, the average medical student feels compelled to strive for perfection. Each time we correct something done wrong and improve our technique, we move a step closer to what we believe will be perfection, the correct treatment. Medicine today requires great expertise in order to deliver technical competence. In achieving these skills the profession has shifted from one of blessing to one of shaming and not only in physician training.

Physicians are not intentionally malicious, shaming people. Quite the opposite, the men and women attracted to careers in medicine are by nature caring and compassionate. But technology moves with momentum. In their earnestness to do a good job in ever finer arenas of technology, they have become focused in their heads.

Modern life opens a path not to the soul but to the shopping mall, and the force of growth has been diverted onto this path.

- Eliot Cowan

Changes in medicine are being made from the marketplace, while perceptive thinkers have issued calls for social responsibility and offered guidelines to evaluate the goals and results of treatment.[15] The cost of medicine has driven it into the arms of managed care where corporate principles of business management allocate resources. Treatment is now focused on algorhythms and guidelines. These can be useful and powerful. A non-medical example is that an airplane pilot and her passengers benefit from the landing check list, which provides a reminder to put the "wheels down" before putting the plane on the runway. Similarly a patient and busy physician can both benefit from an organized treatment approach that helps to guard against key steps being overlooked. On the other hand, my experience with treatment guidelines and the committees which draft these documents is that this paper work is not capable of helping physicians lead patients to the transformation of purpose or wisdom. This higher level of insightful care and healing perception is not created by a bureaucracy or institution.

Today decisions are dollar driven and filtered through an avalanche of algorithms, regulations, and rules. Most of these regulations are well intended, but collectively push the physician through fear of reprisal, more and more into a mind place. The savings resulting from the burgeoning science and corporatization of managed care has been at the price of taking the heart and joy out of medicine. Many can see that something important is missing. But the search is directed further into the process of creating more bureaucracy and regulation. In a desire to promote better health in this era there are many suggestions advocating performance monitoring[16] while acknowledging that health depends on many interactive factors. One suggested direction is for governmental public health agencies to increase their ability to oversee providers and managed care organizations thereby ensuring the public's health through additional regulation.[17]

Despair not; the paper work that feeds the bureau-

....the awareness unit, the human soul.

- Torkom Saraydarian

*The lack of meaning
in life is a soul
sickness whose full
extent and full import
our age has not yet
begun to comprehend.*

- Carl Jung

cracy of managed care has been computerized into a paperless process. I was talking with friends about these aspects of medicine one evening, when I began to laugh thinking of what Schweitzer would say today. In the 1950s he apologized to Norman Cousins for the fact that he had been unable to talk one afternoon. He pointed to a pile of forms placed on his desk. "All this is to be filled out," he said. "Now the French government has asked us to prepare complicated forms for each patient at the hospital. Miserable paper work. Also now we have to fill out workmen's compensation forms for the working people who come to the hospital. Dozens of items for each patient. And I hardly know what to do with these." Schweitzer confided, "My paper work is killing me."[18] I said to my friends that if the paper work was burdensome for Schweitzer in the 1950s he would not believe what medicine has become today. More energy is funneled into the forms and regulations and less and less directed to the patient.

An unfortunate consequence of all this is the imposition of timetables for patient recovery. When someone is not on schedule with the regulations, they begin to experience pressure from all involved in their care, including their insurance carrier for not being "normal." Patient education can become a sermon: shame on you for not eating your vegetables. Shame on you for drinking too much, for not wearing your seat belt, for not walking or jogging enough today. Shame on you for being late. You are not good enough. You don't measure up.

*Plant trees so birds
can sing for
generations to come.*

- R.G.H. Siu

How can it be possible to grow and learn to trust yourself, if no one ever believes in you and your relationship with the community? Can medicine and the world of technology regain a balance between blessing and shaming? That would require a model of health which we do not have, but which can be built on the concept of the 'right to be.' Chapter 4 describes existing components for a model of health that exist within the mainstream culture. These components have been selected because they encourage listening to your heart.

The idea of teaching a child to listen to her heart may sound foolish to mothers and fathers preparing youngsters to succeed in the competitive world of today. However, teaching the path of the heart is an affirmation of the 'right to be a part of the whole.' Listening to the heart does not preclude careful reasoning and thinking, but rather brings an additional value dimension with which to make decisions. The heart without careful reasoning and logic may be pulled by feeling alone and fail to see important factual realities. Decisions must be sound and arrived at with all the relevant data. Ignoring the knowledge base available for sound decisions or pursuing flawed thinking may put your life and health at risk. While the mind organizes and processes a situation, the heart is doing a value assessment. Sometimes they may struggle to find agreement, but as Eddie Box, Sr, Ute elder, says, "The mind searches the possibilities and then the heart decides."[19]

My path is the way of the heart My task is healing.

- Gretchen Bering

Solomon wrote "a heart at peace gives life to the body[20] and a cheerful heart is good medicine."[21] He warned, "above all else guard your heart for it is the wellspring of life."[22] This wisdom of the heart transcends the muscle which pumps blood and is indeed the life spirit by which we live. Conversely, the risks and consequences of a hardened heart have long been known. The consequences of a mind running ahead without the body, emotions, and essence can be disastrous

In retrospect ....we were wrong, terribly wrong. We owe it to future generations to explain why.

- Robert McNamara

regardless of how brilliant the intellect may be.

Traditional Chinese medicine saw the heart as the supreme controller of a being.[23] We evidence this in our culture with such sayings as, "He did it, his heart was totally in it" or "It didn't happen, his heart wasn't in it." But the Chinese took it further. The acupuncture points of the heart meridian originate at the "utmost source" in the arm pit and extend down the arm to the little finger. The energy which we send out from our heart, surfaces at the "utmost source"and travels down the arm and out into the world. We must be prepared to sort out what comes back so that we take in and absorb only what is safe and nourishing. Not everything that comes to us should become part of us. Otherwise our heart and eventually our whole being are at risk of being overwhelmed or poisoned. Positive energy attracts negative energy.

When our sense of values is not balanced with infinite and timeless values, we lose our path and work for our own destruction.

- Torkom Saraydarian

The second acupuncture meridian is small bowel, the "sorter" which comes up from the little finger along the arm and shoulder to the head. It separates the pure from the impure, that which we want to take into our being from that which we want to discard and eliminate as waste. Sorting and screening the people and experiences which come to us can be carried on at an intellectual level where we evaluate with reasoning the logic and soundness of information. Testing with the heart is a qualitative evaluation. Heart in the traditional Chinese culture implies heart-mind consciousness. Ancient universal qualities such as trust, kindness, patience, mindfulness, simplicity, humility, and honesty enable us to go beyond the hardness and blockages of the heart. By being true to our heart we support our journey.[24] If our heart is closed off we are unable to receive and integrate the information of our soul.

Attempts to open a heart from the outside will always be unsuccessful. Trying to convince someone by statistics, argument, or coercion to open his heart will fail. A famous painting portrays Christ knocking at a door. The painting is complete in all details, except that there is no handle on the door at which he knocks. The artist was asked about this omission and he replied that it was not an omission, the door of the human heart has no handle on the outside and must be opened from within. The heart can be closed as a result of an old wound, by arrogance, or lack of discernment. A receptive heart accepts teaching and grows wise. But no one can give spiritual knowledge to another, for that is already within each person's heart. A teacher or physician can kindle the light hidden in the heart. But if the light is not there, it is not the teacher's fault. "However great be the teacher, he is helpless with the one whose heart is closed."[25] This wisdom crosses all cultures, "Where the heart is willing, it will find a thousand ways, but where it is unwilling it will find a thousand excuses."[26] Sometimes the unwilling person is troubled by doubt and this is understandable today.

We know that God not only loves you but has selected you for a special purpose.

- 1 Thessalonians 1:4

Doubt

I don't have all of the answers. I am familiar with doubt and confusion. They are companions when I travel into unknown territory. I have had to make an alliance with doubt. It is a safety device to keep me on track, but not to stop me. Doubt is always with me, an ever-present human frailty. It warns me I am in unfamiliar terrain.

Doubt can easily be reinforced by the culture. If reverence for my 'right to be' is not greater than my doubt

The marvelous peculiarity about admitting to being lost is that we come to our senses.

- David Whyte

(or if shame is added to my fear), I am at risk of giving up the rhythm of my heartbeat.

This ever-present human frailty of doubt does serve to keep me from becoming an egomaniac. But when I am ill, injured, shamed, or wounded doubt may become overpowering. Overwhelming doubt can become a negative pre-occupation.

Schweitzer knew that the people of this century are not rooted in a trust of themselves and their own thinking. The culture itself promotes self doubt and lack of trust. Advertisers and marketers thrive on our insecurity, to get us to buy or try any new thing. The inevitable individual doubt, which is our traveling companion, is fed by cultural doubt.

Today, in addition to . . . neglect of thought, there is also a mistrust of it. The organized political, social, and religious associations of our time are at work convincing the individual not to develop his convictions through his own thinking but to assimilate the ideas they present to him. Any man who thinks for himself is to them inconvenient and even ominous. He does not offer sufficient guarantee that he will merge into the organization.

Man today is exposed throughout his life to influences that try to rob him of all confidence in his own thinking. He lives in an atmosphere of intellectual dependence, which surrounds him and manifests itself in everything he hears or reads. It is in the people whom he meets everyday; it is in the political parties and associations that have claimed him as their own; it pervades all the circumstances of his life.

By the spirit of the age, then, the man of today is forced

The answers cannot be found outside oneself; they must come from within.

- Kat Duff

into skepticism about his own thinking, so that he may become receptive to what he receives from authority. He cannot resist this influence because he is over-worked, distracted, and incapable of concentrating. Moreover, the material dependence that is his lot has an effect on his mind, so he finally believes that he is not qualified to come to his own conclusions..

His self confidence is also affected by the prodigious developments in knowledge. He cannot comprehend or assimilate the new discoveries. He is forced to accept them as givens, although he does not understand them. As a result of this attitude toward scientific truth he begins to doubt his own judgment in other spheres of thought.

Thus the circumstances of the age do their best to deliver us to the spirit of the age. The seed of skepticism has germinated. In fact, modern man no longer has any confidence in himself. Behind a self-assured exterior he conceals an inner lack of confidence. In spite of his great technological achievements and material possessions, he is an altogether stunted being, because he makes no use of his capacity for thinking. It will always remain incomprehensible that our generation, which has shown itself so great at its discoveries and inventions, could fall so low in the realm of thought.[27]

Schweitzer observed this dilemma in 1931. His speaking in Aspen did not change the flow of events. He lived in a period of spiritual decline for mankind.[28] Now sixty-six years later, the current is even faster and swifter. We are in it. The flow is all around us, it guides and molds American thinking and lifestyle. In the realm of lifestyle, corporate advertising is the dominant educational institution in our country.[29] "A

Sacredness is a perception based upon one's level of awareness.

- David Cooper

generation of youngsters has been trained to regard nature in a way that coincides with corporate objectives."[30] The American way has become the way of the world, but it does not honor and affirm reverence for your life, the life of others, or the life of nature. If we are to awaken to Schweitzer's wisdom, we need understandings and experiences that penetrate our hearts with enough inspiration to help us claim and nourish our 'right to be' rather that feeding our doubt.

Taking away the sacred 'right to be' of any individual not only creates doubt, it is the soul death of shame from which we seek to recover as individuals, as a culture, and now as a planet. This is why Schweitzer's concept of reverence for life is so difficult for us, whether we are talking about our own children or the salmon in the Columbia River. We have shame-based cultural, educational, and medical systems to name only a few. Cultures which we have judged as primitive and inferior, are not shame based, but in fact, honor and bless the sacredness of each child, adult, and all of nature. Owning one's sacredness is a perception that changes the core value of a being. The violence of denying sacredness manifests through people and creatures across our land and around the earth. Meaning is absent when the sacred is absent. Meaninglessness is equivalent to illness.[31]

In traditional cultures meaning is everywhere. Not just in human affairs but in all of life. For thousands of years people of the earth have seen trees as powerful symbols of meaning.

The image is of a continual movement, an exchange of energies along the trunk of the tree, between root and crown.

- Paul Jordan Smith

Tree of Life

The tree is a universal sacred symbol for life, providing meaning and inspiration to people for thousands of years.[32] It must continue to grow in order to stay alive. Trees can take root at high altitude in the places where shallow pockets of soil collected after the glaciers retreated from the granite. Roots can find cracks in the rock to penetrate deep into the earth. Branches reach toward the sun. The winds of weather and change bend the branches and may even break them. The life of the tree is moving above and within the earth in a total commitment to growth and survival. The tree reaches toward the resources that sustain its purpose: water, soil, minerals, and sunlight. It draws them and receives them.

Like a tree, our lives are shaped by the interaction of the internal and external forces influencing our growth. Our core in this modern life opens onto a path not to the soul but to the shopping mall, the force of growth has been diverted onto this path. The result is our contribution to economic growth—the conversion of nature and trees into things. We call this the "gross national product" and unless it is growing every year, our economy founders. The only escape from this out of control growth is to rediscover that material growth is a youthful phase which prepares the way for the real growth into 'eldership.'[33] The difficulty is that there is not much support to rediscover real growth. All media seems to glorify, even worship youth, and the culture seeks to prolong youthfulness. Elders are not valued, but rather thrown onto the scrap heap as soon as their prime consumer years are over. Many people resent the assumption that they were born to shop.[34] I remember vividly the day a woman in Grand Junction spoke in a dialogue, she realized that her culture had educated her to be a consumer. A long silence followed in the sacred circle as we each reflected on her realization and integrated this understand-

It may be that some little root of the sacred tree still lives. Nourish it then, that it may leaf and bloom and fill with singing birds.

- Black Elk

ing. The resentment she felt was healthy anger, for it provided the power needed to cleanse and overcome the obstacles to claiming her soul and purpose.

The materialism of Aspen in 1949 was modest and primitive compared with today's excess and opulence, but even then Schweitzer was asked if American "materialism" is a barrier to participation in spiritual things. He emphatically said, "No, beyond material things one goes through to the spiritual and behind the spiritual things is often found materialism."[35] Materialism is a youthful phase which we outgrow if we wake up spiritually.

Trees are traditional sources of inspiration and spiritual meaning. The tree gives life and protection to all men and women. The shade of the tree shelters us from the sun. Trees provided the framework for the branches, hides and mud that covered the roof and walls of the first dwellings.[36] The tree provides wood for the fire giving protection from the cold. Because of the "standing people," trees, men and women are able to stand in shelter. Medicines and tools come from the branches of trees and plants.

When you see each leaf as a separate thing, you can see the tree, you can see the spirit of the tree, you can talk to it, and maybe you can begin to learn something.

- William J. Bausch

People saw in trees a symbol of the great laws of universal motion: the cycles of life and death. That which is above is mirrored below. The connection of heaven with earth was represented by the cosmic tree. The sacred tree was the center of the world and its consecration. Ancient people saw in every tree the connection of the earthly with the divine. Its roots penetrate into the depths of the darkness to give strong support and the crown of the tree strives toward the light with its unfolding branches. Ancient men and women could open up in trust to this knowledge of the tree.[37]

For all of the people of the earth, the Creator planted a sacred tree under which they might gather, and there find healing, power, wisdom, and security. The roots of this tree spread throughout the earth. Its branches reach upward like hands praying to the sky. The fruits of the tree are the good things the creator has given the people: teachings that show the path to love, compassion, generosity, wisdom, respect,[38] and altruism. In Delta, Colorado, there stands an aged cottonwood, the massive Ute Council tree, in the protection of whose shade people gathered many years ago to speak in council, with respect.

At the edge of the river where I walk is a great tree. A ponderosa, my arms reach barely half way around. The spring high water of the runoff has exposed some of its roots so that I am able to see a small part of what is otherwise invisible in the ground. There is mystery in the earth under the tree, which I can feel. Relationship with the earth and nature has been one of the traditional sources for divine inspiration and meaning. The tree is inherently whole: roots, trunk, and branches are a unitary structure with a total commitment to its 'right to be.'

*Man is a tree
of the field.*

- Deuteronomy 20:19

Commitment

"It is up to each individual to claim her right to be," says Tu. A tree or animal doesn't struggle with doubting its right to be, but sometimes I do. Doubt came with the package. With continuing to talk with my essence the doubt can come into balance. When an alliance is made with doubt, it becomes a traveling companion, which is no longer disabling because there is an effective strategy. Doubt in such a relationship is an ally. We all have had the experience of learning a

*As soon as you
trust yourself,
you will know
how to live.*

- Goethe

new skill. Before we achieved competence we doubted whether we would be able to throw the ball through the basket. Once we did it and made the commitment to practice, we became confident. Even when we missed shots, we were not discouraged from trying again. Continuous perseverance over time characterizes a commitment.

With commitment I am able to work and play without being eroded by doubt. I can commit to a turn on a bicycle or pair of skis. Hesitation, a lack of focus, or succumbing to a distraction can all be devastating at the critical moment of weight transfer. That is a lack of total commitment. A disastrous fall can occur if the timing is off or all of the parts are not cooperating and performing together.

Once the commitment is made the process can become easier. The continual adjustments necessary to maintain my balance are no longer difficult. This is beyond the beginning level of awkward weight shifts. Once the intention is there to commit to the process and the successful corrections are made to maintain balance, a sense of confidence replaces doubt. The emotion is now joy, no longer fear. I can ride my bicycle down the hill and around the curve. I am able to ski this slope under control.

With commitment to a working process, a sense of trust begins to develop. Doubt is no longer disabling, but helpful. I wonder if there is gravel on the road; that curve could be dangerous with gravel on it! I will slow down. Doubt has become an ally. My essence can now hear when doubt is speaking. This new snow is wonderful, but I wonder what the avalanche danger is back here behind the ski area?

Safety

When I respect myself, I am able to extend respect to others. Reverence for the gift of my life rises from my soul and is experienced as a perception in my mind and heart. I am sacred with a right to be a part of the whole. Reverence for life, begins with knowing the inner sacredness of myself and extends throughout the space I occupy. There is a light given to me by my Creator. This light is my gift to the world and my responsibility. Being conscious of my light requires that I protect myself. For life feeds on life. Life is in many ways a drama that can be described as survival of the fittest.

The sacred call is transformative.

- David Cooper

As I honor the light of my essence, I must keep it safe and shielded. Claiming my 'right to be' requires aggressively protecting my sacred space and self, because I live in a culture that does not revere my 'right to be.' This culture knows about competition. It does not know about reverence for life. The media conspire together to convince a child that if she doesn't compete to win, she will be a loser. Cooperation from a place of reverence is known only to a few spiritual communities. In our competitive culture we place a high value on reason and convincing arguments. If those methods do not succeed more violent techniques can be effected.

The world is a dangerous place. "The man who mistrusts himself will mistrust even his best friend; the man who trusts himself will trust everyone."[39] As I learn to trust myself I cannot afford to be naive or foolish. Although a trustworthy friend will not likely attack me, there are many people who do not know respect and some will attack. Danger is ever present and you will be confronted by those without spiritual

*To injure an opponent
is to injure yourself.
To control aggression
without inflicting
injury is the
Art of Peace.*

- Morihei Ueshiba

*The battle to keep
the world in balance
rages continually.*

- Joel Monture

awareness and values. The teaching to extend love in the face of fear is correct, but you can only do this from a place of keeping yourself and your life safe. Know that not all people look upon you with reverence. Some will violate you.

Frantic frightened people in overcrowded conditions will bump into you or verbally try to push you off balance or out of line. The machine culture does not move at a rhythm which is healthy for you. Human beings have feelings and values, corporations do not.[40] They are guided by the values of the people who operate them. Even if you are on the right track, you will be run over if you are not going fast enough. Being aware enough to know when to step out of the way is an appropriate way to protect yourself. In the presence of someone who is unconscious of his own sacredness, do not give up reverence for your own 'right to be.' Stay safe.

The first and easiest step in staying safe is to be a neutral observer. We do not need to engage with all of the chaos and confusion in the world around us. The second step is to blend with the aggressive energy, redirect it to a neutral place and release it as one is taught in the martial art of aikido, deliberately and with focus. The third step is to engage in conflict only as a last resort. There are critical moments when the 'right to be' is under attack and to give up that right is to turn down the flame. Eventually, the light can be put out, and we can become an empty shell, living without light. When under attack, Morihei Ushiba the founder of aikido advised, do not stare into the eyes of your opponent he will mesmerize you. Do not look at his sword it will frighten you. Don't focus on your opponent at all. Hold space for yourself and who you are and he will feel that.[41] To carry that awareness, surrounded with a shield of respectful dance and play-fulness, can be lighter and more fun than traveling with heavy armor.

When I ask a patient to extend his arms and mark the boundary of his containment field, he is usually able to accept that this is his personal space. When I say this is your sacred space, he may nod his head and accept this as well. But when I say to him, "You are sacred" there is often a hesitation, a questioning and some may ask, "Is that alright?" People tend to doubt their 'right to be,' their sacredness, and their own thinking. They need acceptance and reassur-ance in order to claim their 'right to be.' I ask if they believe the Creator is the source of the animals, mountains, rivers, and trees. I ask if they believe that the Creator made them. When they begin to trust their thinking this much, they can begin the journey of listening to their heart. As they begin to trust their heart, they begin to experience joy. "Health increases your joy."[42]

Your spirit is the true shield.

- Morihei Ueshiba

Pilgrimage

As I commit to claiming my 'right to be,' a trust and a confidence begins to grow in my ability to safely walk with reverence for myself and all life. Walking the path is now more than a physical exercise. The jour-ney has become a sacred one; life is a pilgrimage. Spiritual travelers the world over are known as pil-grims—not just those people who landed at Plymouth Rock. All of our parts are with us on the journey and we find support in many ways. "To walk a sacred path is to know and trust that there is a guidance to help us live our lives on this planet. Guidance can come in many, many ways."[43]

*A man's soul can only
travel as fast as his
feet can carry him.*

**- Old Native
American saying**

When the path to health is seen to be a pilgrimage, the essence is with us on the journey and we are working with all our parts. We are now connected to the abundance and mystery of the universe with gratefulness. People of the land belong to the earth. This is a different concept than owning the land. People who walk in a relationship of belonging to the earth evolved a way of life where they ask permission before they harvest or take and express thanksgiving, in gratitude for that which they received. Once this subtle change takes place, a cycle of fullness and wellness accompanies the harvest, rather than the emptiness that can quickly follow eating, shopping, or taking when nothing is given back in gratitude.

Similarly, when walking on the land with an attitude of respect and gratefulness, both life and travel become a pilgrimage, which is very different from the tourist who comes to a sacred mountain, river, or valley but only takes and never gives back. A pilgrim comes in reverence and thanksgiving and honors the cycle of reciprocity. Rupert Sheldrake, an English Biologist, was asked where he would begin to effect change in the world. He said, "I would change tourism into pilgrimage, help tourists become pilgrims."[44] What would be necessary for that to happen? We would need to look native people in the eye and apologize. We would then need to request their cooperation to re-consecrate places in the land where we might go as pilgrims. That will be a big step. You can effect an equivalent local change in your life today and build a bridge from medicine to health. Make it your intention to listen to the rhythm of your heart and claim your 'right to be a part of the whole.'

Trusting that you have a 'right to be,' even in the presence of aging changes, cancer, degenerative intervertebral disc and vascular disease, is to own your inherent power. This is an awesome power and trust. "How few in the world know trust. What is necessary is not trusting another, even the teacher, but oneself, and one is not capable of trusting oneself fully when one has not experienced in life how to trust another."[45] "Lack of trust is weakness. . . . It is with trust and confidence in God and in that divine spark which is in one's own heart that one is assured of success in life if one will only step forward."[46]

As I learn to trust myself, my respect and reverence for both myself and others increases. Each day when I go to the river my respect for a small dark bird increases. As I write this it is winter and yet water ouzel is still here. Many other birds have gone south but each morning my courage is nourished by ouzel. She is similar in shape to a robin, but smaller, with a short stubby tail. Slate gray almost black in color. On overcast winter days ouzel is a little darker than the water of the river. She has my greatest respect— despite the frigid winter temperatures, hopping and plopping into the flowing river to retrieve bugs, small fish, and worms. She jumps out onto a water-covered rock but is not swept away. On the rock she dips up and down, again and again, and then dives. She is able to avoid washing downstream in the current while searching for food. Her intention to survive is a total commitment in the harsh winter. There is no doubt in ouzel's movements as she claims her 'right to be.' Ouzel, I thank you for the inspiration and clarity of purpose which you show me.

As I move through the silent aspen grove deep in the winter snow, I give thanks to you standing beings who capture and hold the warmth of the sun. Your wood gives warmth to my hut. I give you thanks for the oxy-

I give you the end of a golden string; Only wind it into a ball, It will lead you in at heaven's gate, Built in Jerusalem's wall.

- William Blake

*The Tree is an
apparently simple, but
ultimately extremely
complex chart detailing
the descending
emanations of
the worlds.*

- Eliezer Shore

gen you give to me in the summer. I give thanks that you make my life possible. I extend to you respect for your 'right to be.'

My community is growing to include people, creatures, and trees for all of whom I have reverence. As I welcome them, I am received into a relationship of sacred space.

Chapter 4

The Community of Sacred Space

Connecting the rhythm of your heart with the
rhythm of the earth and sky will keep you in
touch with the natural cycles that keep
you healthy.

Tu Moonwalker

How does one keep a sane rhythm and pace of life in
this frantic harried culture? It is not easy, but I find it
helpful to regularly set aside time to connect with the
rhythm of the earth. Winter is a season of quiet,
reflection, and stillness. Spring is a time of warming
and new beginnings. Summer calls for the cultivation
and loving care of new growth. Autumn is a celebration of the harvest with thanksgiving. Connecting the
rhythm of my heart with the rhythm of the earth is a
lot more fun than racing somewhere on a crowded
highway. When possible, a walk in the woods with a
friend by the creek is more joyful. When my 'right to
be' moves with the rhythm of the earth, I am able to
release the steering wheel. Balance and calm can be
remembered, and my relationships with people
become friendlier and warmer. Being in rhythm with
the earth has a healing effect. Being in community
with people, animals, or plants is a powerful health
influence.

*The healing of
ourselves is the
healing of the
whole nation.*

- Thich Nhat Hanh

Relationships are vital to health. Even without an
awareness of 'the right to be a part of the whole,' there
is research evidence that health benefits accumulate
for individuals who form meaningful social ties with
other human beings. A web of affirming human relationships is known to nurture and protect an individ-

*One's action ought
to come out of an
achieved stillness;
not to be a mere
rushing on.*

- D. H. Lawrence

ual. People lacking meaningful relationships, or experiencing a breakdown in relationships experience adverse effects on their health.[1] Considerable evidence exists from studies in Alameda County, California, where community and social setting were shown to have a positive health benefit. The same type of beneficial correlation is known to exist for people in relationship with animals. One study demonstrated that owning a pet was the most important factor in predicting a patient's clinical condition following a heart attack. This was more important than coronary risk factors such as smoking, high blood pressure, high blood cholesterol levels, or diabetes mellitus.[2] Likewise, it is widely agreed that caring for a plant gives an opportunity to succeed at something positive and increase the quality of life.[3]

Attitudes and Being

Attitudes and beliefs influence behavior and health.[4] My belief and perception of 'a right to be' for myself has enlarged and extended from myself to others. The concept has now become 'a right to be a part of the whole' for myself and all others, every being that lives. My community beliefs and needs adjust accordingly. My definition of community has grown beyond the dictionary description of a social group of any size whose members reside in a specific locality. I am now seeking something additional.

The process of moving beyond an individual perception to a collective 'right to be a part of the whole' calls for a collective intention of respect to be held by the whole community. Social experiences are needed for growth and purpose to develop in healthy relationship with other human beings and the natural world. A community is created when people agree to come together because of a shared intention. Holding the intention for each person in a community to claim a 'right to be a part of the whole' is an achievable challenge in the American culture of today. To create such a community, focus first on the modest initial steps of walking with respect, speaking with respect, and seeing with respect. These represent an ambitious undertaking, and will allow community bonding and networking to grow organically. Out of this can grow a cooperative flow of meaning.

I behave in accord with how I perceive a situation. If my experience and perception only know a competitive culture, I will not have the experience or skills with which "to be" in a community of respect. A community with the intention of supporting each other's 'right to be a part of the whole' has distinguishing characteristics. It is altruistic. Individual health needs a social context, where creativity and the capacity to change are accepted. Life is not static. A safe place is necessary in which to make the awkward movements and steps necessary to risk growth. This requires that the growth be organic. To be a community that respects 'the right to be' requires a space which is not dominated by competitive behavior. It must be a place where it is possible to risk an awkward step forward toward growth without being subjected to competitive or shaming attack. A sacred space sets a boundary within which it is safe to claim 'your right to be a part of the whole.'

In a competitive situation the need to do and perform in an aggressive manner dominates behavior. This setting is not necessarily safe for new growth or creativity. In an affirming culture a network of collaboration and support is fostered. Optimally, life is a

It is not the mountain we conquer, but ourselves.

- Sir Edmund Hillary

Only in Soul-awareness do you taste the beauty of joy.

- Torkom Saraydarian

healthy balance between its competitive and cooperative aspects. The competitive calls forth my strengths, which need to be available in order to meet a challenge, while the cooperative nourishes and supports me in evolving and maturing. We live in a competitive culture and world. However, a culture that models health also requires an atmosphere of acceptance and affirmation.

Competition

Throughout nature and communities there is always competition. Competitiveness is an important part of the whole. Life feeds on life. The community needs the strengths of our gifts and talents. The American way is competitive and this can bring forth the best in us. We seek to exceed everyone else and outrun the competition. That competitiveness is basic to our business, education, medicine, military and wealth. Competition has an important place, but it gets out of balance when a sufficient boundary around aggressiveness does not protect cooperation. When the mind overrides the soul with negative messages, when the parent shames a child, or when an employer devalues a worker, a boundary has been violated. If we only know how to compete and are unable to hold a field of affirmation (blessing) and cooperation, we fall into a state of conflict. Conflict with ourselves and with others. A consequence of too much competition is a fracturing off of parts of ourselves, as mind from body or as in political or social organizations, as blacks against whites or men against women. Excessive splintering into separate fragments which are unable to cooperate is unhealthy. Synergy atrophies.

In a culture that primarily knows competition, we struggle to stay ahead of the shame of defeat. Many of

What grows in solitude then goes back into the community.

- Ruth Cooke

us learned to try and outrun the devouring jaws of shame through doing more. My ability to do many things and accomplish many tasks became the source of my self esteem and value. When I did not know blessing for my 'right to be' I became aggressive. Competitive success inflated my arrogance and kept me from feeling shame. But this path was a lonely isolated one and did not lead into an affirming community. A healthy community accepts my frailties, as well as my strengths.

How I align my power is critical. Selfish power is well known for its ability to corrupt. Our education and experience have taught us to be uncomfortable with power. We find our wariness confirmed by the abuses and excesses of many politicians, corporations, and even religious institutions. This kind of power becomes a vicious god to serve. This is the power of the small self, manipulating others. Or the process by which others manipulate us, when they have power over us. These conditions shut down both creativity and growth. They literally pull your essence out of you. In contrast, there is the power of our essence and wholeness affirmed and aligned to the Creator within a sacred community. This is when the quest for the higher Self becomes the quest for God. An example is the first principle accepted by the members of Alcoholics Anonymous when they acknowledge that they are powerless to overcome their problem. Their first act is to align themselves with a "higher power." This place of resignation and surrender, "no self," is the place where God is encountered—self transcendence.[5] This is one of the great struggles of a lifetime to subordinate self-will to a higher voice and purpose. The Swiss psychiatrist Jung said he was not so much concerned with the treatment of neuroses as with the approach to the supernatural. His experience was

Life is meaningless without the knowledge of our divine identity.

- Andrew Harvey

that the problem of every patient who came to him over age thirty five was one of finding a spiritual outlook on life, and no one was healed until he gained this outlook. Wholeness can only be achieved through the soul (essence).[6]

We are involved in an array of relationships ranging from family, to the people we live and work with, to our Creator. While the path of selfish power is dangerous, the solution does not reside in powerlessness, which is less than a full life. Rather, the goal is empowerment in accord with divine guidance and purpose. There is a need for a healthy relationship of balance between competition and cooperation—each individual claiming and living their 'right to be a cooperative part of the whole.' In the human realm we experience three different types of people power: the power of the individual, the power which other people and institutions have over us and the collective power which people have together.[7] The collective power of people in a community is proportional to their ability to cooperate.

Christ said, "Don't be afraid of those who try to kill your body, but of those who try to kill your soul." He did not did not curse us and say be powerless, but rather, "You are the light of the world. . . . people do not light a lamp and put it under a bowl. Instead they put it on a stand, and it gives light to everyone in the house."[8] This light is not the power of selfish greed, but rather is illuminated by a power greater than ourselves. This radiance needs cooperative human relationships within a sacred space. A supportive and cooperative relationship with ourselves and our community enables a higher level of function and health than an environment which is only competitive and threatening. When someone or an organization holds

Essentially, the process of initiation removes our Ego from the center of the universe.

- Robert Moore and Douglas Gillette

threatening power, it becomes more difficult for people to hear the rhythm of their heart. In those conditions we experience manipulation and are working against a challenge. How we view the opportunity to meet a challenge and make choices is totally different if we are dependent and powerless. The empowerment inherent in the 'right to be a part of the whole' is a part of the gift of life. Powerlessness manifests as unnecessary disability, dysfunction, and social isolation. A community with the intention to affirm 'the right to be a part of the whole' sets a protective boundary and contains itself within a sacred space.

Organizing energy and relationships of community in a sacred manner is very different from a solely competitive model. We can gain useful insight from members of communities where the intention to balance cooperation and competition still survives. Just as Schweitzer found the inspiration for "reverence for life" in Africa, we can find inspiration for community from some locations on that continent today. Fortunately, within mainstream American culture there are learning organizations and processes where it is possible for you to claim your 'right to be a part of the whole.' Organizational structures exist where it can be safe to walk, speak, and see with respect. While these organizations and processes do not actively espouse the 'right to be' they offer the type of cultural soil where the rhythm of your heart can take root and begin to grow. The 'right to be' can become the collective intention of a community. For the model of how elders relate in support of the 'right to be,' I will return to the inspiration and words of the native people, for their League of the Iroquois is the form of political relationship which we have chosen for our democratic government. However, our model is incomplete without the contribution coming from the

To be in a machine like culture is to have one's soul constantly at risk of being sucked out.

- Malidoma Patrice Somé

strength of each individuals 'right to be a part of the whole.' For incorporation of this component will require respect for cooperation as well as competition.

There is much confusion in our land today. We and the other industrialized nations have lost the tradition of affirming and empowering children and individuals in our community. Today the corporation and its products are valued and promoted. Products are honored. But in traditional villages native people considered themselves and their community continuous with the sacred earth.

Community

Malidoma Patrice Somé, an African, writes of his village experiences of affirmation and initiation into a role of responsibility. Even when distant from home his community has committed to support his teaching and working in America. Away from his village he feels continuing acceptance and affirmation. "Without a community you cannot be yourself. The community is where we draw the strength needed to effect changes inside us."[9] A community is formed each time more than one person meets for a purpose. The development of community depends on what the people involved consent to be their intention. What is acknowledged in the formation of a community is the possibility of doing together what is impossible to do alone.[10]

"This acknowledgment is also an objection against the isolation of individuals by a society in service of the Machine. What we want is to create community that meets the intrinsic need of every individual. The individual can finally discover within the community

In the absence of the sacred - nothing is sacred - everything is for sale.

**- Oren Lyons,
Onondaga Tribal
Chief**

something to relate to, because deep down inside each of us is a craving for an honoring of our individualism."[11] Deep down inside each of us is a craving for our 'right to be' and to do. We need a community to affirm us. "A community is a place of self-definition."[12] "Any group of people meeting with the intention of connecting to the power within is a community," by Somé's assessment. He writes of his work with Americans who want a means to relate to each other—a means that has nothing to do with what shopping centers afford them.[13]

"A true community begins in the hearts of the people involved. It is not a place of distraction but a place of being. . . . In community it is possible to restore a supportive presence for one another, rather than distrusting one another or competing with one another. The others in community are the reason that one feels the way one feels. The elder cannot be an elder if there is no community to make him an elder. The young boy cannot feel secure if there is no elder whose silent presence gives him hope in life. The adult cannot be who he is unless there is a strong sense of presence of the other people around. This interdependency is what I call supportive presence."[14] This is the cooperative and supportive intergenerational presence which Maslow witnessed as the young child struggled to open the cabin door in the Blackfoot village. (See Chapter 3)

What is so good about being together with each other is that we can each be the starting point for the possibility of building a larger community. Formation has to happen in a nurturing way if it is to work and prove itself to the rest of the world. In other words, it has to prove itself to be different, attractive, and nurturing without the ambition of competing with the current

A joyful society is a healthy and prosperous society.

- **Torkom Saraydarian**

dysfunctional communities supported by an army of policemen.[15] In order for this to happen, an organization or structure is necessary to create and hold a sacred space. The only way I know to hold and integrate the tension (balance) between competition and cooperation is to walk a sacred path.

Walking: Labyrinth

Walking a sacred path is an ancient notion. Motivation is what separates a pilgrim from an ordinary traveler.[16] A medieval European tradition of sacred walking follows a geometric circular pattern called the labyrinth. The meditative use of this path leads each of us to our own center. "Nurturing ourselves spiritually is not an easy thing to do in a culture that disconnects us from our depth."[17] The simple act of walking quietly in a sacred manner invites us back into the center of our being.

It is an old ironic habit of human beings to run faster when we have lost our way.

- Rollo May

The labyrinth helps people to "see their lives in the context of a path of pilgrimage. They realize that they are not human beings on a spiritual path but spiritual beings on a human path. To those of us who feel we have untapped gifts to offer, it stirs the creative fires within."[18] "All of the world religions contain teachings that articulate the journey of the spiritual seeker; the path one must walk in order to grow in compassion and respond to the world with clarity and wisdom. In essence, the task is to grow the "substance of the soul."[19] The labyrinth can be a tremendous help to quiet the mind, because the body is moving. Movement takes away the excess charge of psychic energy that disturbs our efforts to quiet our thought process.[20]

The Chartres Cathedral Labyrinth

Often the labyrinth is not walked in solitude but with other people, so that there is an experience of continually meeting people on the narrow walkway. This affords the opportunity to step aside or pass someone walking more slowly in a sacred manner. These simple experiences quietly speak to my heart, and my whole being changes. A container is built to organize and hold the energy of a group walking a sacred path.

When I am walking by the river or on the ridge in a sacred manner and meet another pilgrim traveling toward me, we often pass with only a word, a gesture, or even in silence. The experience affirms the sacredness of each of us. An accentuated moment of joy and wholeness travels through us and around us as we respectfully acknowledge

I have told you this so that my joy may be in you and that your joy may be complete.

- John 15:11

the other. It is an acknowledgment of reverence for the other's 'right to be' that gently and immediately cycles back to the giver. On the river a similar experience can occur. I may float past a camp and pass within a few feet of others, but both of us remain silent. Choosing not to disturb the sacredness and stillness of the canyon, we nod quietly in greeting. Traditional communities have known how to travel in a sacred manner for thousands of years. They also know how to speak in a sacred manner.

Speaking: Dialogue

Our voice has more power than we know.

- Ellen Draper and Virginia Baron

My words are my most powerful medicine. The words I speak to myself and to others may be either healing or wounding.[21] The ancient form of sacred communication was a council. This has been the tradition not only of indigenous people, but also holds a place of respect in classical Greek culture.[22] David Bohm suggests that council or dialogue is a stream of meaning, flowing among and through and between the people participating. He contrasts this with the words "'discussion which has the same root at 'percussion' and 'concussion.' It really means to break things up. It emphasizes the idea of analysis, where there may be many points of view, and where everybody is presenting a different one—analyzing and breaking up. That obviously has its value; but it's limited, and it will not get us very far beyond our various points of view. Discussion is almost like a ping-pong game, where people are batting the ideas back and forth and the object of the game is to win or to get points for yourself. Possibly you will take up somebody else's ideas to back up your own. You may agree with some and disagree with others, but the basic point is to win the game. That's very frequently the case in a discussion."[23]

"In dialogue, however, nobody is trying to win. Everybody wins if anybody wins. There is a different sort of spirit to it. In a dialogue, there is no attempt to gain points, or to make your particular view prevail. Rather, whenever any mistake is discovered on the part of anybody, everybody gains. It's a situation called win-win, whereas the other game is win-lose—if I win, you lose. But a dialogue is something more of a common participation, in which we are not playing a game against each other but with each other. In a dialogue, everybody wins."[24]

A contemporary example is the form of communication evolved by computer programmers. A model for the organization of a computer program is called a "pert chart." Many, many component parts need to be correctly programmed in order for the whole system to function properly. If there is a mistake anywhere, the system will not work optimally, or often not at all. This has necessitated a form of communication which promotes locating "bugs and errors" without subjecting programmers to the experience of shame or loss of self esteem. When someone takes on shame they shut down. Their light doesn't shine. Their creativity and talents don't flow. A shame based communication system doesn't promote writing successful software. Computer programmers do just the opposite of concealing their mistakes. Instead of hiding errors or feigning perfection, they celebrate when an error is found, because when the "bug" is out, the system will function better.

I believe much trouble and blood would be saved if we opened our hearts more. I will tell you in my way how the Indian sees things. The white man has more words to tell you how they look to him, but it does not require many words to speak the truth.

**- Chief Joseph
Nez Perce**

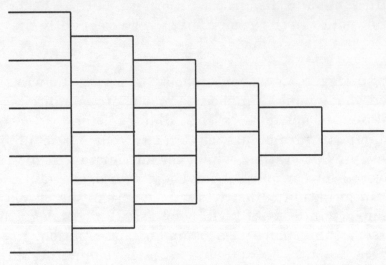

A Pert Chart

Their culture has developed "egoless programming."
They suspend judgment to effect better communication. They make an alliance with the fear of making
mistakes, by acknowledging that everyone makes
errors. The community agrees that the fear of mistakes will not allow shame to smother their talents or
obscure "bugs." As a result their work, their product,
and their relationships take on a different meaning, a
healthier meaning for them and their software.

What is dialogue? In my experience most dialogues
begin with a time of silence. Silence was meaningful
for the Lakota, and his granting a space of silence
before talking was done in the practice of true polite-
ness and regardful of the rule that "thought comes
before speech."[25] The Quakers are also respectful of
the power that can fill a space of silence. A Quaker
might say, "When we listen devoutly, the heart
opens."[26] These moments of silence slow things down
and create a separation from earlier times and places.
People gather in the present moment, sit in a circle,

and speak one at a time. This is both time-consuming and exciting. In a sacred space one can speak without being interrupted. One can be heard. It is enlightening to listen without a need to convince or convert. When we slow down our thinking, we can allow ourselves to be more inclusive and fluid in our thoughts.[27]

The modern form of dialogue, articulated by physicist David Bohm,[28] was developed at the MIT Sloan School of Management. Isaacs relates a significant story he was told of a dialogue-type process. Late in the 1960s, the dean of a major U. S. business school was appointed to chair a committee to examine whether the University should continue to design and build nuclear weapons on its campus. People on the committee were in an uproar over the issue. The chairman had no idea how to bring all of these people together in agreement on anything. He changed some rules and said that the committee would meet every day until it had produced a report. Every day—weekends, holidays, everything. "You can not do that," people said. He responded, "Yes we can. We will continue to meet. If you can't be here, that will be okay."

The committee eventually met for thirty-six continuous days. The first two weeks they had no agenda. People talked about anything they wanted to talk about—the purpose of the university, how upset they were, their fears, and their noblest aims. Eventually they turned to the report they were supposed to write. By this time the people had become quite close to one another.

To the surprise of some, the group produced a unanimous report. They agreed that the university should phase out the building of weapons. This was not a consensus process in the traditional sense, but rather an

The voice carries the emotional body of the person speaking.

- **David Whyte**

The voice, like the eyes and the face is traditionally a window to the soul.

- **David Whyte**

agreement on a direction, for a variety of reasons. Some people felt the laboratories were extremely expensive and administratively complex; others felt the presence of weapons was morally wrong. The important lesson which showed itself here was that people did not have to have the same reasons to agree with the direction that emerged.[29] A flow of meaning emerged from a setting where people spoke and listened with respect.

Dialogue inherently creates a safer mode of communication than competitive discussion which can often become confrontational, explosive, and fragmenting. Dialogue can help to create openness and community where people are able to experience a safe place of support. Peter Senge who with William Isaacs, was instrumental in introducing the dialogue concept to private business interests says, in the 1994 Introduction to his popular book, The Fifth Discipline, "We see this openness very clearly in the research of dialogue, a basic element of team learning, which has been conducted over the past two years at MIT. The research began as a tentative exploration of a radical approach to improving conversation within practical management situations. Guided by rediscovering the origins of the "dialogue"—the Greek *dialogos,* "flow of meaning"—and by the pioneering research by Bohm and others, the project started by establishing several on-going dialogue groups. Before long it mushroomed. Dialogue groups are forming in a wide variety of settings in the public and private sector. But it is the impact this work seems to be having on people that has been the most surprising. We are learning that there is deep hunger to rediscover our capacity to talk with one another. . . ."

"An ongoing dialogue involving all the key partici-

Intelligence is the ability to prosper and create an environment.

- Page Bailey

pants in the health care system of a middle size Colorado community over the past two years has led to deeply moving observations such as this comment by an administrator: 'We have always believed that the doctors were basically lording it over everyone. I am beginning to see how much they too are suffering in the current system. People literally hold them responsible if a loved one dies.' Recently, the head of one of the hospitals in the community suggested that perhaps his organization should be merged with another hospital, a traditionally bitter rival, 'for the best interest of the community as a whole'."[30]

"Dialogue is like an electromagnetic field. If you observe a scattering of iron shavings on a paper and then place a magnet underneath, you will witness a "magical" alignment as magnetic energy "flows through" from magnet to shavings. In dialogue, meanings flow through the group, propelled by the energy of open conversation, creating a collective field of alignment."[31] "Dialogue helps us to share our most honest thoughts and feelings skillfully and respectfully, as we learn to "speak from the heart" rather than from our rehearsed or established routines. The beliefs, attitudes, thoughts, and feelings that stem from our mental models and cultural influences color our experience of the world and our relationships. Sometimes we discover that our beliefs and experiences do not coincide with those of others, creating gaps of understanding and respect, and preventing us from moving forward together.

When we face those challenges, most of us default to one of three reactions: fight, flight, or freeze. We might *fight* hard for our views, believing we can move forward only by prevailing over our opponents (or obliterating them). This approach does little to create

Contrary to popular myth, great teams are not characterized by an absence of conflict.

- Peter Senge

*Reckless words pierce
like a sword, but
the tongue of the
wise brings healing.*

- Proverbs 13:18

synergy, may prevent the best idea from emerging, and can damage our relationships. We can *flee,* avoiding confrontation, and letting someone else win, which can have the same effect. We can *freeze,* shutting our mouths in non-committal silence, judging the others but being unwilling to play the game.

Whether we discharge haphazardly or hold it in until we burst, unskillful communication can pollute our relationships like so much toxic waste. It can also prevent us from moving forward as effectively as we might wish. Through dialogue, however, a group can learn to hold disparate, seemingly irreconcilable views in a state of "suspended animation," allowing them to be present without attachment or without giving them up. Instead, the participants can explore the reasoning, emotions, and desires behind each perspective. Such respect and intention toward understanding often creates the unexpected possibility of experiencing the collective articulation of new truths."[32]

In traditional cultures, dialogue is called council. This has become the preferred term in school settings, where the process has become popular with young people. Writing about the mystery of council in school groups Zimmerman and Coyle say, "It is difficult to write about what happens in Council. As is true for other timeless ceremonial forms that are still actively evolving, Council works its magic in mysterious ways. . . . Current time dissolved and we had the distinct feeling of being nourished with the wisdom of an ancient circle of elders gathered to make an important tribal decision. . . . The feeling of interdependence of the circle was visceral and carried with it a sense of our inseparable connection with both past and future. The council seemed to have an evolutionary life of its own; a life whose presence we felt palpably at the time, even though describing it now eludes our powers of articulation. This sense of interdependence can extend beyond time and familiar environment to include other cultures and even other species. A diverse group can become a microcosm of larger ecosystems made up of animals, plants, and land-scapes. We come to see each person in the circle as representing another culture or species, intrinsically valuable for her unique presence. When this occurs, we glimpse our humanity, no matter how important, as part of a larger organism and so realize a profound sense of connectedness with other forms of life."[33]

The circle of people sitting in a field of council or dialogue create what is called a container. Dialogue is not without controversy. When differences of opinion occur in a group, this creates instability in the field. If the container is strong enough the group can withstand the instability and often a new creative insight or inspiration evolves, which no one had seen before.

This does not occur spontaneously, but rather results from the leadership and collective intention of the circle. When emotions begin to surface and conflict enters the field, that is when the elders and holding capacity of the container are tested. When sufficient altruism and wisdom is present it is possible to extend acceptance and the 'right to be' in the face of fear and anger. That is when creative energy and a new sense of meaning flows through the circle to transcend individual fear or anger. Rather than leading to fragmentation and withdrawal the group behavior becomes characterized by purpose, synergy and unity.

In business organizations different levels of authority may be present in the same container. It is essential that the field of dialogue be held with sacred integri-

When we begin finally to risk telling about who we really are .... we can come home.

- Angeles Arrien

ty for when people risk speaking their truth they will feel violated if people with power over them do not respect their vulnerability and abuse this power differential.

The story of dialogue has been going on for many thousands of years. Its re-emergence may be a signal that the capacity for collective intelligence is the next step in our evolution—and an essential step for our journey together to continue to unfold.[34]

My experience is that dialogue can shift the hearts and minds of people.[35] One of the great gifts for me in dialogue has been to see the beauty of other people as they speak their truth in the circle. People who are allowed to open their hearts and grow in a field of support began to flower. Speaking in this way can open one's eyes to seeing in a sacred manner.

Science is rooted in conversations.

- Werner Heisenberg

Seeing: Resiliency and Assets

I would say that the Blackfoot Indian respected the child more than the American observer.

- Abraham Maslow

Seeing the gifts and strengths of yourself, a child, another adult, or a creature in the woods can become a way of looking with respect. The Blackfoot who taught Maslow about respect, saw a child whom they knew could open a heavy cabin door. They saw ability not disability. Looking at assets was more rewarding than looking at age, size, or weakness. Researchers are now finding the same thing.

The most well known of these investigators may be Emily Werner, who in 1989 reported in *Scientific American* a thirty-year research study of the 698 children born on the island of Kauai in 1955. The purpose of the research was to assess the results of adverse child-rearing conditions on children's overall develop-

ment. Despite poverty, discordant home life, unedu-
cated, addicted, or mentally-ill parents, one third of
these high-risk children went on to develop stable
work careers, healthy personalities, and strong inter-
personal relationships. Werner identified protective
factors that "have a more generalized effect on the life
course of vulnerable children than do specific risk factors."[36] Resiliency is the positive capacity of someone
at risk to succeed despite adversity.

Resilience is a combination of closely related abilities
that seem to work together to produce the capacity to
bounce back and recover from a challenge, disap-
pointment, obstacle, or setback.[37] The attributes of
resilient children include responsiveness, flexibility,
empathy, caring, communications skills, a sense of
humor, and prosocial behavior. Resilient children are
more responsive, more active, and more flexible and
adaptable even in infancy.[38] Among these protective
factors is one consistent finding—the ability of these
children to recruit one adult who believed in them.
Werner says, "They were easy-going, lovable kids who
recruited people who helped—and they gave something back to the adults who interacted with them. It
is most important the children encounter people (not
programs) who foster their competence."[39]

Other researchers and studies are further document-
ing the power of resilience and finding that most children, who grow up with the odds against them, successfully overcome adversity. They had or developed
the resources to bounce back despite obstacles and
hardships. This perspective focuses on how human
beings adapt and stay healthy.[40]

For young people the Search Institute headed by
Peter Benson has developed a list of "assets"—com-

*Let us remember
To respect
Many ways of learning
And how many paths
Toward wisdom
There may be.*

**- Oral history of the
Oneida People
Paula Underwood**

*True places are not
found on maps.*

- Herman Melville

mitments, values, and competencies—that help an individual to thrive and be responsible.[41] He advocates an approach that accents healthy development of youth through a framework of developmental assets. These forty building blocks are needed by children and adolescents to grow up to be competent, caring, and healthy.[42] When the assets are present, there is research evidence that young people are protected from risk-taking behaviors and positive behaviors are nurtured and valued by society. This program recognizes and seeks the participation and support of all adults in the community, not just parents.

The assets are categorized as to external assets, such as positive developmental experiences that surround youth with support, boundaries and expectations, and opportunities for the structured use of time. The internal assets include the internal strengths, commitments, and values young people need to guide their choices, priorities, and decisions. They are grouped into categories of educational commitment, values, social competencies, and positive identity.

*Each time we
experience a sacred call,
we are instantly drawn
into our true nature.*

- David Cooper

The carefully studied city of Albuquerque, New Mexico, showed that 81 percent of 6th- through 12th-grade students in the public schools had a sense of purpose. This was the most widely held asset in 12,440 students surveyed. This strength may speak to the innate resiliency of youth and the human capacity to be optimistic about the future, even in the face of evidence to the contrary.[43]

Benson knows that language shapes consciousness, and he chooses his words carefully. He has carefully selected forty assets which correlate with healthy youth. These assets were derived from councils with Navajo and Zuni elders, as well as from his comprehensive knowledge and review of the scientific literature.

Seeing: Mindbody as a Unitary System

For chronic illness and recovery from accident, injury, or surgical procedure, Page Bailey has written a curriculum-based course of study to guide nervous system process toward health. This classroom program is an authentic healing field directed toward helping people with chronic conditions in recovering. Bailey's work is applicable to all people seeking more meaningful and healthy lives. A classical scholar, student of modern physics, and master teacher, Bailey has blended a sound understanding of both learning theory and psychoneurophysiology. The science behind the class takes a student into vigorous study of how healing capacity and potential can be activated. This can strengthen and support a positive shift in physiology and create an improved recovery experience within anatomic and biochemical limitations. The nervous system has an endless capacity and a continuous demand for information and experience. This activity needs guidance. No division is made between mind and body, rather students are immediately taught "mindbody" is a unitary system. A major focus of the study is on the importance of understanding the role of meaning in illness and health. Students learn that there is a continuum from meaning, to being, to emotion.[44] "Your mind is your steering wheel."[45] Bailey teaches people how to work with their assets and resiliency and regain control of their steering wheel.

He teaches that meaning is physically active and "we award too much power to our stressors and too little to ourselves. We tend to give too much power to our stressors and too little to our own coping skills. We also tend to forget, during periods of high stress, that we can develop new coping skills and eliminate negative coping skills. Successfully dealing with new

Life provides you with healing opportunities. It is up to you to find them.

- Page Bailey

To each is given the manifestation of the Spirit for the common good.

- 1 Corinthians 12:7

stress levels often requires the development of new coping skills."[46] The patient becomes a student in order to study and implement knowledge therapeutically. The student is also inspired by the progress witnessed in their resilient peers, because they are learning in a field of respect and safety. The person who does the work and makes meaningful progress becomes an exemplar.

This approach to health is called Educotherapy, and it respects the patient's 'right to be.' However, because it seeks to cooperate with all forms of medical care it calls out for a bridge connecting it with the existing systems for treating pathology. The bridge needs to be built from both ends. From the teachers, like Page Bailey, who understand learning theory and nervous system guidance, and from the clinicians treating disease and pathology. Patients who become students in this system learn how to turn on this pivot point from being a victim of a chronic condition. It is not mind over matter or an attitude control, but a scientific means of equipping the patient with an effective strategy for directing the nervous system's capacity. Teachers and physicians are encouraged to bridge the gap with communication and education, as well as medical care. When they support the patient's innate capacities and strengths with meaningful information and understanding, the victim role falls away. Patients become students of their own health because they inherently seek and want to more effectively guide their nervous systems in ways that will strengthen the recovery of their 'right to be.'

Fortunately, Fred Kofman and Peter Senge are carrying these perspectives and skills forward into the business and corporate world, with "learning communities"[47] and "learning organizations."[48] The central

When your concepts change, your experience also changes.

- Page Bailey

concept of moving toward "personal mastery" is described as: starting with "clarifying the things that really matter to us, of living our lives in the service of our highest aspirations. . . . As such, it is an essential cornerstone of the learning organization—the learning organization's spiritual foundation," writes Senge.[48] "Personal mastery" is more than competence and skills, although it is grounded in competence and skills. It extends beyond spiritual unfolding or opening, although it requires spiritual awareness and growth. It means approaching one's life as a creative work, living life from a creative as opposed to a reactive viewpoint.[49] Personal mastery has much in common with the 'right to be.'

Senge quotes Henry Ford, "The smallest indivisible reality is, to my mind, intelligent and is waiting there to be used by human spirits if we can reach out and call them in. We rush to much with nervous hands and worried minds. We are impatient for results. What we need . . . is reinforcement of the soul by the invisible power waiting to be used . . . . I know there are reservoirs of spiritual strength from which we human beings thoughtlessly cut ourselves off. . . . I believe we shall someday be able to know enough about the source of power, and the realm of the spirit to create something ourselves. . . . I firmly believe that mankind was once wiser about spiritual things than we are today. What we now only believe, they knew."[50]

Organizations will learn only through individuals who learn. Individual learning cannot guarantee organizational learning. But without the individual, no organizational learning occurs. People with a high level of personal mastery are continuously living in a learning mode. It becomes a process and lifelong dis-

We can have fire in our approach only if our heart is in the work, and it is hard to put our heart in the work when most of what we feel is stress.

- David Whyte

A life that honors the soul seems to have a kind of radical simplicity at the center of it.

- David Whyte

cipline.[51] 'Personal mastery' is the MIT version of the 'right to be a part of the whole.' These programs use dialogue as the preferred mode of communication to extend respect and open the vision of people to the gifts and talents of themselves and each other.

In all of these systems: pilgrimage, dialogue and assets, recovering, resiliency and learning programs, a network of relationships begins to develop into a community of nurturance and support. Authentic, healthy community can be promoted because an intentional field of cooperation and respect exists, as well as the inevitable field of competition.

Relating: Mentors and Elders

A mentor is one who affirms and supports another person's balanced strengths and capacities as pertaining to their health and usefulness. Good mentors are continually being mentored by their students. Each is involved in giving and receiving in the cycle of reciprocity.[52] An elder is a person who has come to a maturity, which enables them to be concerned not only with their own children, but all children. They represent an ideal of a positive possibility of maturing in a community. In the past, elders have been understood to be wisdom holders of experience that worked and that which did not. A new elder is emerging who can do the former and also in a diversity of styles own the fullness of their gifts and wisdom, and guide this development in others during a time of great change.

*Commit yourself to
your own
personal mastery.*

- Peter Senge

Elders tend to congregate and cooperate with each other. A healthy community is not led by one person alone, but is guided by a council of elders seeking balance, truth, and beauty. The League of the Iroquois was a council acting in a democratic fashion. A similar collective system was noted in the early 1500s when one of Francisco Coronado's soldiers wrote that the Zuni had no chiefs "but are ruled by a council of the oldest men" whom they called *papas*. The Zuni word papa means "elder brother," and each clan elected its papa the way the Iroquois clans did. The women had the vote.[53] Elders think of the whole community, and they think a long way ahead.

> Think not forever of yourselves, O Chiefs,
> Nor of your own generation.
> Think of continuing generations of our families,
> Think of your grandchildren
> And of those yet unborn,
> Whose faces are coming from
> Beneath the ground.
>> Words spoken by the Peacemaker,
>> founder of the Iroquois Confederacy
>> circa 1000A.D.[54]

"In our way of life the Elders give spiritual direction. The wisdom of thousands of years flow through their lips." speaks Mathew King, Lakota.[55] "God gives us each a song. That's how we know who we are. Our song tells us who we are. . . . Everyone (has) got to find the right path. You can't see it so it's hard to find. No one can show you. Each person's got to find the path by himself," says Charlie Knight, Ute.[56] "I just wasn't cut out for the age we're living in. Everybody's hurrying but nobody's going anywhere. People aren't living, they're only existing. They're growing away from spiritual realities. These days people seek knowledge, not wisdom. Knowledge is of the past; wisdom is of the future. We're in an age now when people are slumbering. They think they're awake, yet really they're sleeping. But this is a dangerous age, the most dangerous in human history.

Each soul must meet the morning sun, the new sweet earth, and the Great Silence alone.

- **Ohiyesa Santee Sioux**

Know thyself.

**- Inscription carved
on the facade of the
temple of Apollo
at Delphi**

*Old age was simply
a delightful time, when
the old people sat on
the sunny doorsteps,
playing in the sun
with the children,
until they fell asleep.
At last, they failed to
wake up.*

**- James Paytiamo
Acoma Pueblo**

People need to wake up. They can't hear God's voice if they're asleep." Vernon Cooper, Lumbee tells us.[57]

The Iroquois confederation became the model for the Congress of the United States. The current Iroquois confederation is still looking ahead. "In our way of life, in our government, with every decision we make, we always keep in mind the Seventh Generation to come. It's our job to see that the people coming ahead, the generations still unborn have a world no worse than ours—hopefully better. When we walk upon Mother Earth we always plant our feet carefully because we know the faces of our future generations are looking up at us from beneath the ground. We never forget them," says Oren Lyons, Onondaga.[58] Telling about how wisdom was found by a man after many years of searching, "He finally learned that wisdom comes only when you stop looking for it and start truly living the life the Creator intended for you," says Leila Fisher,[59] Hoh. "Let us live in peace and harmony to keep the land and all life in balance. Only prayer and meditation can do that." speaks Thomas Banyacya, Hopi.[60]

The wisdom keepers teach that the future is not some abstract, untouchable 'beyond' far out there somewhere, outside our knowing. Rather the future is here with us today, in the Now and Here.[61] "Every part of this country is sacred to my people . . . the very dust responds more lovingly to our footsteps than to yours, because it is the ashes of our ancestors," said Chief Seattle.

These elders have lived their lives owning their 'right to be a part of the whole.' That gives their beingness a living connection with all of nature. They accept and bless the 'right to be' for seven generations. Confidence grounds their wisdom. "The right to be" gives you the right to make mistakes. With mistakes comes wisdom. To own the 'right to be' is to give yourself the chance to survive with all of the accumulated experience of wisdom. The 'right to be' gives me the right to go forward and see the future. It is then my prerogative whether to step forward or not.

The choices necessary to step toward health require that we walk, speak, see, and relate in a way that calls forth purpose and blessing for seven generations to come. What I hear from wisdom holders is that we all have a 'right to be a part of the whole,' but the path and times of life are difficult now. As we take each step we are responsible for thinking long term and holding true to what is best for all concerned including ourselves.

A wisdom holder from our culture was Jonas Salk. He knew that this epochal change is stressful and observed that humans are being tested for the attributes which will be favorable to our health and survival.[62] It was his belief that the attribute of greatest importance for this challenge will be wisdom, a new kind of fitness.[63] For this humans will need to be able to join feeling and reason, nonverbal and verbal, as well as subjective and objective sources of information and problem solving. He said that wisdom will necessitate the ability to make judgments in advance rather than retrospectively.[64] Salk saw that the future will be one of *survival of the wisest.*

Man's greatest experience - the one that brings supreme exultation - is spiritual, not physical.

- William O. Douglas

How does wisdom function within medical care and research? The popular culture has chosen to equate medical care with health by using these words interchangeably, but is this true? Certainly medical care and science are helpful and important parts of the whole.

To understand how medicine and health might wisely cooperate we need to step out of the community of sacred space and into medical history.

CHAPTER 5

MEDICAL CARE AND HEALTH CARE

> You can't make a cat out of a dog.
> Jonas Salk

There is a traditional Hebrew folk tale about a group of physicians gathered around a table. As they sipped from their cups, they fell to arguing about which part of the body, and therefore which specialty, was most important for life. They could not agree among themselves and decided to consult the rabbi.

Great labor cannot be carried on alone. A great labor is a team work.

- Torkom Saraydarian

"Of course the heart and blood vessels are most important," said the cardiologist, "for on them the whole life of man depends."

"Not at all," said the neurologist. "The brain and nerves are most vital, for without them, even the heart would not beat."

"You are both wrong," the gastroenterologist said. "The stomach and digestive passages are most important, for without proper digestion of food, the body will die."

"The lungs are most important," declared the pulmonary specialist, "for a man without air will surely die."

"You are all wrong," said the rabbi. "There are actually two vessels of the body that are important, but you have no knowledge of them."

"What are they, then?" asked the physicians.

The rabbi replied, "The channel that runs from the ear to the soul, and the one that runs from the soul to the tongue."[1]

The soul was in trouble from the beginning of modern medicine when it could not be found in the anatomy lab or under the microscope. Modern medical care is based on pathology. Pathology is the science which deals with the nature, causes, and development of abnormal conditions,[2] which we call disease. Medicine has two traditional functions: to prevent disease from developing and to cure disease once it has occurred. The major medical triumphs of this century have involved both approaches. Improved sanitation, housing, nutrition, and immunizations prevent the infectious diseases which were the major causes of death in 1900. In the last half of this century, antibiotics have become effective in reducing mortality from infectious diseases. This two pronged assault on infection has reduced deaths and disability from this ancient enemy of health.[3] These achievements have been made possible and effective through the accurate identification of the problem at its source and scientifically evaluating therapy until an effective treatment is proven, by controlled clinical studies. The triumph of antibiotics is representative of the strategy which has resulted in the stunning medical and surgical successes of today. The focus of medicine is on combating pathology.

This orientation developed over centuries of careful attention to the injuries and disorders which patients experience. But this perspective evolved slowly. Traditional medicine did not come from an understanding of pathology, but rather from a spiritual ori-

Disease and episodes of sickness remind people that meaning is an achievement.

-Lawrence E. Sullivan

*....our soul is the part
of us that picks up on
situations well ahead
of our conscious
awareness of them.*

**- Malidoma Patrice
Somé**

entation. The original healers lived in awe of creation, and their treatment was directed toward supporting and restoring a patient to a harmonious *relationship* with self, community, and nature.

This tradition still lives today in parts of the world; in America, its vestiges are with the native people. Traditional medicine holds man in a holistic view of Oneness with the Creator, man is a part of the earth. The basic belief is that the solution to problems resides in the wisdom of the heart. The soul aligned with the Creator is the source of the inspiration, ideas, and vision that bring healing, light, and meaning to life. The soul is the bridge between body and spirit and helps us as mediator or connector.[4] Disease and distress from the traditional perspective were disorders of imbalance, and the original medical practitioners as well as those who continue this work today treated patients from a spiritual perspective. Traditional medical practice did not distinguish between medicine and religion. When therapies and herbs were identified that could help problems, these treatments were assimilated and the knowledge was passed by oral tradition to an apprentice. As effective interventions were identified the patient continued to be treated in a spiritual environment; always with relatives, friends, and community present and involved, since they were considered a part of the condition.[5]

Medicine's turn away from the spiritual toward the scientific explanations and treatments for disease is credited to Hippocrates, about 400 BC.[6] His teaching and approach led to a more accurate physical understanding of dysfunction. Galen, another famous Greek physician, who followed Hippocrates by about 600 years, carefully studied anatomy. He gained important experience as physician to the gladiators, who suffered horrible wounds and came under his care. Galen's medical views were a blend of rational scientific observation and the Greek theory of the four humors: blood, yellow bile, black bile and phlegm. His approach persisted until the 16th century and began to decline in the 17th century.[7]

There was an invention in 1590 comparable in cultural impact to the computer of today. It was the microscope. Zacharias Janssen, a Dutch spectacle maker, and Galileo have both been accredited with inventing this instrument.[8] Neither of them could have had any idea of its effect on the course of history. With its revolutionizing power people could look into a world that had never before been seen. What was revealed changed medicine forever. The microscope made possible the examination of human tissue, cellular changes, and bacteria. With further technical development and refinement, chromosomes, intracellular structures, and viruses could be studied.

In the absence of the sacred - everything is for sale and life has no value.

- Anne Wilson Schaef

By the 18th century, Morgagni had demonstrated with the aid of autopsies that disease began in specific organs of the body.[9] Rudolph Virchow (1821-1902) was able to follow principles of scientific research with the microscope to arrive at the understanding that cells are the basic units of life, and that disease can result from disturbances of the cell's living processes. With Virchow's research and teaching, cellular pathology began to dominate biology and medicine.[10] Pathology continues to hold this prominence today. Virchow's most brilliant pupil was named von Recklinghausen.[11]

In April of 1876, a young American physician sailed for Europe and arrived in Strasbourg to study in von

Recklinghausen's laboratory. His name was William Henry Welch. Modern American medicine recognizes Welch as its founding father, for he established the first pathology laboratory on this continent in 1878 at Belleview Hospital.[12] With more precise understanding of pathological processes, the etiology of many disorders were accurately discerned and understood. From pathologically based medical practice and research have flowed specific and effective modern medical practices, management, and surgical treatment of disease.

Medical practice evolved from Hippocrates, who taught high levels of self-responsibility for healthy behavior, but provided a comparatively low level of physician effectiveness in treating physical illness and trauma. In contrast a late twentieth-century medical practice provides high level physician capacity for the care of injury and trauma, but a relatively low level of physician effectiveness in teaching patient responsibility for self care and health. (With the realization of the role of self responsibility in chronic conditions, the importance of patient education is again being widely acknowledged. But this teaching is not yet based on respect of the patient's 'right to be.') Today, lifesaving capacities are the expected norm and current capabilities have become truly powerful. Technical analysis, diagnostic, surgical, and therapeutic methods have exploded in complexity and effectiveness. Development of the pathologic interventive model is accompanied by the transfer of more and more authority and responsibility to the medical doctor. Accordingly, the patient's 'right to be' has diminished. With the increasing effectiveness of understanding disorders from a pathological perspective, the mind and soul have both lost presence and power in the life of the patient and physician. The modern

Nothing so concentrates experience and clarifies the central conditions of living as serious illness.

- Arthur Keinman

physician searches for pathology. If no pathology is found, there is no disease and the treatment is reassurance, "nothing abnormal on the lab work from the pathology department," is the comforting phrase that signals that, "nothing needs be done."

The Limits of Scientific Diagnosis

Despite its benefits this approach overlooks significant conditions which do not yet manifest identifiable pathology. The subtle signals of internal mental and physical distress and disease can be ignored. The pain of meaningless work creates an imbalance which will slip past physical biochemical analysis for some time. We perceive that the traditional medical practitioner was less effective in techniques for dealing with significant pathology. While the modern medical doctor has become less effective with disorders of the mind, essence, and our imbalances with the community and nature. A modern physician is never trained in how to affirm your 'right to be.' Respect for the rhythm of a patient's heart beat is innate only to a clinician who lives and practices in attunement with to his own heartbeat. The strength and wisdom of the traditional approach has not been joined to modern practice. In fact, the gap widens and the failure of the two domains to connect and cooperate has adverse consequences.

The physician is only the servant of nature, not her master. Therefore it behooves medicine to follow the will of nature.

- Paracelsus

Each of these two medical views are inherently powerful as evidenced by the staying power of traditional medicine and the success and growth of the pathologic model over the past two hundred years. A posture of exclusivity, where one system dominates the other, lacks the strength of cooperative unity which would be possible with the benefit of both perspectives.

America has not made this synthesis, and is dominantly invested in the allopathic, pathologic model and exclusion of traditional wisdom. Because medical doctors are taught that traditional medicine lacks scientific proof, there is no measurable alignment with the power of nature and the culture of wisdom holders. Without scientific verification, wisdom is left out of the laboratory and out of the operating room. Without wisdom, the highest use of science is the most cost-effective treatment of disease. The unifying world view of the United States melting pot boils down to economic profit from capitalism. A casualty of this outlook has been respect for the individual 'right to be.' The cultural view of health has evolved to a pathologic definition: health is the absence of disease. The dilemma is not that medical care is wrong, but it is incomplete. This view is limiting without a foundation in wisdom that values the individual essence and purpose. Without the soul there will not be an authentic model of health no matter how aggressively we market self responsibility.

To ward off disease or recover health, men as a rule find it easier to depend on healers than to attempt the more difficult task of living wisely.

- René Dubos

The Body Without the Soul: the Machine

How did we get here? If the value system that guides a culture in the use of technology is not consciously held in view all of the time, that ideal will be lost. If an organization or community is not continuously affirming the wisdom of reverence for life, respect for the rhythm of your heartbeat becomes a cynical joke on the street. "How many of us really expect to do meaningful work? Get serious."

The invention of the microscope was not intended to diminish the soul. But as the world view changed, a trend began. The world seen through the microscope was so expansive, that strict methods were developed to evaluate what was significant. At the same time, Descartes' power of intellect and world view divided man into mind and body. Man was viewed as only a machine. Over the years trends converged and the soul began to disappear. More rigorous scientific criteria were needed to evaluate what was statistically significant. Prospectively controlled, double-blind experiments became the "gold standard" for what would become the accepted standard of care. The essence failed to satisfy the investigative criteria. Scientific research has not confirmed that human beings ever had or needed an essence or purpose. As more value is placed on scientific validation and less on wisdom, the relationship of the soul to purpose has been devalued. Whether any one person intended to take the soul out of medicine, is impossible to know. But when it was no longer continuously acknowledged, along with its disappearance faded the 'right to be a part of the whole.' That core philosophy had held the connection between the strengths of the individual and the community. Without this bridge from the individual to the community neither the dominant culture nor the pathologic medical model can present a meaningful model of health. The lack of wisdom in understanding the word "health" in "health care reform" is evidence of this confusion. This soulless perspective comes into conflict with what everyone from children to poets have known and said for years.

An example of medical scientific perspective is represented by Lewis Thomas, the highly respected President of Sloan-Kettering Cancer Center for many years. Thomas believed in the realization that disease can be turned around by treatment, provided one only knows enough about the underlying pathology[13] and that this knowledge alone will enable us to begin thinking about a society relatively free of disease.[14] As

To follow up this vision which we have seen, to keep it in mind when we are thrown back again on the world, to live in its light and to shape our lives by its law, is to wind the string into a ball, and to find our way out of the labyrinth of life.

- Bede Briffiths

sensible as this logical world-view may sound, the emotional and economic reality of chronic disease and disability manifesting from people's meaningless lives tells us that when the soul is absent, life goes empty—regardless of what science has proven to itself.

Traditional wisdom holders come from spiritual roots. The diverse spiritual beliefs of today's culture and the freedom of religious choice established by the founding fathers precludes that there will be a unifying spiritual view in this land. The benefit is that each of us is supposed to have the freedom to find our own path to the Creator. One of the consequences of this freedom has been the loss of the sacred from the collective community view. This together with a medical view that health is nothing more than the absence of pathology has left people with little support from physicians for connecting with a meaningful life purpose. Medical care offers potential rescue from pathology by intervention. But medicine is unable to restore a meaningful and useful life to a person who has never claimed it.

*.... Medical science ...
is full of mysteries,
and must be studied
like the words
of Christ.*

- Paracelsus

On the other hand, spiritual awareness does not insure medical competence in the pathologic management of a lesion. Knowledge and skill in the treatment of pathology does not require spiritual consciousness. But people come into the office bringing their frazzled minds and broken hearts as well as biomechanical diseases. The challenge for the physician is to select the right treatment for the patient. The challenge for a person seeking her 'right to be' through medial care is humbling. Success in a traditional treatment system occurs when the patient is restored to a place of harmony with herself and useful participation in the community. Capacity and useful function are optimized. Success in the medical treatment of pathology is a cure. When this fails to be achieved the opposite of usefulness becomes the focus—disability. In the past, survival was an incentive to struggle and cope despite pain and distress. Today the medical and compensation systems reward dependence, and for some people disability becomes attractive.

Toward Competence with Benevolence

The consciousness can only hold so much information. As the scientist spends more hours looking into his microscope, knowledge and understanding of the microscopic domain increases. Awareness of other domains will decrease. Unless he chooses to also take note of the trees outside the laboratory window and their change with the seasons, these events and others will pass unnoticed. His consciousness will go where he directs it. This can happen to a physician if he sees only pathology. A broader view sees the patient as a powerful and useful person with a 'right to be' and includes an understanding of her disease.

A pathologic diagnosis can too often be incorrectly construed as an impairment that precludes useful participation in the family and community. Disability can quickly result in a meaningless existence. The difficulties of disability and the pathologic model are particularly evident to physicians who see its inadequacies in occupational medicine and the workers compensation system. Western medical care does not have a cure for meaninglessness, and is unable to distinguish whether this symptom develops before or after a presenting illness. The solution and need is to be able to combine medical competence with the ability to support the patient's 'right to be.'

A joyful person is like a dynamo who continuously imparts energy to the hearts of his co-workers.

- Torkom Saraydarian

*The practice of
medicine
is an art,
based on science.*

- William Osler

But in reality, the locus of control today is largely with the medical doctor. Medical care is an external service provided to a patient in a paternalistic relationship at the time of illness or injury. Both patients and physicians understand that the practitioner's action aids a patient's homeostatic mechanisms. Active medical intervention is the physician's response to trauma or disease. He questions, examines, and investigates the patient to locate the pathology. He then prescribes treatment based on what is understood to be the cause of the disease process. The focus of the physician's attention is on identifying what is wrong. Since the 17th century, the practice of medicine has centered on diagnosing the disease that underlies the patient's distress in order to treat symptoms. Dubos referred to this tradition as the "doctrine of specific etiology."[15]

"The dominant model of disease today is biomedical, with molecular biology its basic scientific discipline," says Engel.[16] This is the dominant medical paradigm. This strategy presumes all human distress can eventually be traced to a pathologic lesion whether this is an abnormality in a biochemical process or an obstructed blood vessel. The physician makes a diagnosis and prescribes the treatment he considers best for the problem. In properly selected cases this is highly effective.

The doctor's expertise is what enables a patient to make this leap of trust. Galen, the ancient physician, observed that the doctor "cures most successfully in whom the people have the greatest confidence." This truth still holds in modern medicine, perceptive physicians of today observe that what the patient believes is still of great importance and will influence the outcome and success of treatment.

With the wondrous progress in diagnosis and treatment of disease, patients have placed great trust in physicians. Both patients and their doctors want health. Because of its efficacy the treatment of pathology was believed to be enough. However, when we examine our lives, the benefit is only partial. The history of an actual patient and how the traditional and modern medical models view his treatment can aid in understanding the strengths and weakness of the system we have chosen.

An Example: Carl

Carl was an iron worker, a member of a proud and skilled community. Those who walk and work the steel girders in the sky have a special confidence and ability to labor at heights. Carl came to me as a patient after falling twenty feet to the ground while coupling together steel corner beams of a building. The accident resulted from an error by the crane operator who let a girder fall. Fortunately, Carl was not seriously injured. Examinations and diagnostic studies were performed, and no fractures or disc injuries could be identified. The physicians before me had searched for evidence of what was injured in the fall, but no abnormality could be identified with the newest magnetic resonance imaging methods. Carl complained of disabling back pain and had not progressed in therapy. My consultation was requested.

I prescribed a rehabilitation program for Carl. Unfortunately, the situation had already become confrontational. He was in a contest with the insurance company who was slow in sending his disability payments. He had retained a lawyer and the field was

With rising levels of insensitivity to pain, the capacity to experience the simple joys and pleasures of life has equally declined.

- Ivan Illich

competitively charged. I did not believe he was crazy or that it was all in his head, but that rather knew that he would eventually have to make a decision whether to climb back up onto the steel beams at construction sites. Such a profession requires confidence and a clear sense of who you are. I had never had his experience, and none of my therapists were able to relate to him from that place. He acknowledged his lack of confidence and belief in himself, and talked at length about his fear of being shunned by his fellow workers. "Once you fall, no one wants to work near you." He obviously suffered soft tissue injuries, but his mind and soul had also been wounded. Carl's life had lost its meaning.

Without work all life goes rotten. But when work is soulless, life stifles and dies.

- Albert Camus

In the tradition of native people the focus of treatment is often on understanding and healing a patient's place, relationship, and balance in the community. Restoring his place in the whole must be done in a way consistent with new realities and physical capacities that exist. The medicine societies of the Pueblo Indians of New Mexico are comprised of members who have experienced the problem for which they treat patients. For example, someone who suffers a snakebite or is struck by lightning will be treated by a member of a medicine society who has assimilated that experience.[17] One can imagine the level of understanding and empathy that are possible in such a relationship. The recoveries of other survivors engage an immediate transference and belief rarely accessible to patients today. Meaninglessness rarely developed because of acceptance by the healer and larger community. The 'right to be' was not threatened, it was never questioned. A person was respected and affirmed for functioning and being useful to their community. After an injury, the contribution might be modified, but not voided. Community transforms the experience, as Alcoholics Anonymous and a multitude of similar support groups seek to do in our culture, when there is a commitment to cooperate and an acknowledgment of a higher power.

A Lakota man, who is struck by lightning and survives becomes part of a society whose members were recognized as forever changed, evidenced by the fact that when such a man enters a gathering he will walk in backwards. By our standards, these traditional practitioners have limited ability to treat pathology compared to a physician with the resources of a modern hospital. On the other hand, my own limits in being able to treat the mind and soul of Carl the steelworker were as great. I simply could not effectively approach the traditional level of healing and empowerment. I was unable to connect him with a society of fallen iron workers to support his return to a working community.

As Carl failed to resume iron work he not only experienced loss of income, but loss of identity, marriage, community, and face. My attempts to rehabilitate his 'right to be' were unsuccessful. His community, employer, insurer, and mate could only see what was wrong with him. The MRI was normal, obviously. "It was all in his mind." But they were unable to see how he might claim his 'right to be' and adapt. There was no community to affirm him. They could no longer see his usefulness and began to shun him. In his case, as in many cases, the priority became higher profits, not better health.

Traditional healers know how to transform trauma within the context of the family and community, because everyone is part of the whole and part of the condition. What is difficult for one becomes easier

The patient is entitled to a full mobilization of resources, including his own.

- **Norman Cousins**

when many are moving together with the same intention.

Medicine "assumes disease to be fully accounted for by deviations from the norm of measurable biological variables. It leaves no room within its framework for the social, psychological, and behavioral dimensions of illness," states Engel, who has proposed a biopsychosocial medical model to reconcile mind, body, and society. He argues that a more appropriate medical model must view the patient in terms of a larger context.[18]

Back Pain, for Instance

Few things are more essential for the national future than the need for Americans to be reeducated about health....

- Norman Cousins

The wisdom of his words can be illustrated by the expensive and significant problem of treating people with backaches and back injuries. Back pain is an ancient and widespread human experience. In traditional cultures back pain is considered part of being alive, but not a cause of disability. Today the distinctions between backaches, back injuries, and back disability have become blurred and confused.[19] Never before has low back disability been epidemic. Historically, patients actively sought to cope and stay functional despite their low back pain and physicians supported this effort. Modern physicians and patients can now collaborate on a search for spine pathology. Appropriate treatment of disease in properly selected cases is highly effective. But the discovery of disease has become a source of reward, and in America low back disability is widespread. Frymoyer and Cats-Baril report that low back disability is increasing at fourteen times the rate of population growth.[20] No population is immune to back aches and degenerative changes.

But despite the success of the disease illness paradigm and the many conditions which it enables us to treat effectively, it has limitations which cannot be disregarded. Physicians regularly see people with backaches who do not have a herniated disc. Some low back pain is independent of pathologic derangement. On the other hand, we also know that there can be pathology that does not produce illness or symptoms. In fact, 30 to 60 percent of a normal asymptomatic population under age 35 will have a degenerative lumbar disc[21] and 20 percent of the normal population under sixty will have an asymptomatic herniated lumbar disc on imaging studies.[22] Jensen, *et al,* reported in the New England Journal of Medicine that only 36 percent of 98 asymptomatic subjects had normal discs in the lumbar spine.[23]

Our diagnostic techniques have become so sensitive that we have found that there is much more "spine disease" than we had previously been able to diagnose. Just the opposite of what Lewis Thomas had predicted, at least in the case of low back pain. There is not yet a society free of back disease.[24] In plain English, this means many people tolerate mild pathologic changes and injuries in their spine with little or no discomfort or disability. In fact, the pathology model often fails to predict low back pain. In order to proceed with appropriate active medical intervention for back pain, the physician needs to be able to determine whether a patient's spine pathology is clinically significant; otherwise, a doctor may over-treat and induce an aggravation or unnecessary disability. Telling a patient that he or she has a herniated disc can result in illness-related behavior and absence from work.

An increase in spine disease is not a reasonable explanation for the recent explosion of lumbar disability.

Scientific evidence is accumulating to support the biblical axiom that "a merry heart doeth good like a medicine."

- Norman Cousins

*The connection between
what we think and how
we feel is perhaps the
most dramatic
documentation of the
fact that mind and body
are not separate entities
but part of a fully
integrated system.*

- Norman Cousins

Rather, psycho-social factors are likely the most significant cause. By psycho-social is meant how we feel and learn to perceive and react to a situation. Psycho-social comes from the two words psychology and sociology. The root words of psychology is psyche. Psyche means soul. Its modern interpretation has come to mean not the state of one's soul, but rather the science of mind and behavior, and what go goes "mentally" wrong. So in application to the question, What is the meaning of our work for us? The Boeing aircraft study found that the strongest predictor of low back disability was employee job dis-satisfaction, even more often than physical work factors.[25] Employee work dis-satisfaction is the explanation for disability from a pathological perspective. Whereas from the 'right to be' perspective, disability develops if the essence fails to find a meaningful connection with purpose in work. When soul is not able to align with purpose satisfaction in work is not forthcoming. Sweden leads the world in low back disability, not because of more injuries or increased pathology, but, because they have the highest take-home pay of any nation in the world for those sick or injured.[26] If work is not satisfying, life may become more meaningful at home. The path from backache to disability has now become a highway,[27] and youngsters can learn from the behavioral modeling of their parents. Children of patients with chronic low back pain learn dysfunctional behavior and have more behavioral problems in school than the children of normal or even diabetic parents.[28] This is not intended to diminish the value of appropriately identifying and treating pathologic lesions which can cause low back pain. Much suffering is regularly relieved by skillful physicians, surgeons, and therapists. My point rather, is that patient selection is important, and it is important to acknowledge that the overall medical and surgical management of back pain has not decreased the incidence of low back disability.[29]

Physicians and surgeons involved in spine care today are recognizing they must be mindful that low back pain has a benign self-limited natural history and the rapid increase in low back disability can be best understood with a biopsychosocial medical model.[30] This step of acknowledging the psycho-social aspects of a patient's condition represents progress in claiming neglected parts of the whole. But until the link between the patient's capacities, the soul and 'right to be' is recognized, the psycho-social will have a pathological orientation. In reality, many medical doctors persist with medication first, and if that is not effective consider surgery as the next step, and last, if at all, they turn to education. Because physicians have very little training in patient education, they don't do it often. Talking with people is time consuming and raises difficult issues that most clinicians are simply not prepared to discuss—like essence, life purpose, and meaning. The current treatment plan for low back pain in the context of the social climate, unfortunately, too often results in taking away the patient's power and undermining her 'right to be' and her sense of self responsibility. Because medications are effective in relieving low back pain, it is understandable how a patient comes to believe that the solution is not in herself, but rather in a bottle of pills. In truth, spine physicians and surgeons know the limitations, as well as the benefits of medication and that only a small percentage of patients require surgical intervention. The best outcomes of intervention are achieved in those people who had a meaningful purpose prior to their injury. Treatment of pain and pathology in a patient who has never claimed their purpose is often unsuccessful.

Why should we be in such desperate haste to succeed and in such desperate enterprises?

- Henry David Thoreau

Pain: Who Is Accountable?

Pain is an inevitable part of being alive. Some pain,

*When I suffer pain
I am aware that a
question is
being raised.*

- Ivan Illich

medical care can heal and relieve, but there is much suffering it cannot eliminate. Still, we live in a country where the myth that life should be pain free is perpetrated. That illusion may promote excessive use of medication and unnecessary avoidance of activity and problem solving. That illusion stunts the growth that occurs when we push against resistance or through difficult places. When a muscle works against a resistant weight it is strengthened. So it can also be in working to persevere and solve the difficult challenges, problems, and resistances we face in life. But with dramatic breakthroughs in medical and trauma management, the expectation can be marketed that medical science has a cure for every discomfort, disorder, and disease. This unrealistic expectation has led to an imbalance in patient-physician responsibilities.

The physician is now asked and tempted actively to intervene, often pharmacologically, in areas that are the patient's own health responsibility. The path to a meaningful purpose is not pain free, often there are places of confusion and resistance. The deeply painful "dark night of the soul" is a portal that most pass through on the way to meaning and purpose in life. These issues are educational gaps in the doctor's training. Increasingly aware medical practitioners, meetings, and literature acknowledge the role the patient plays in his own health. They in fact conclude that the major adverse effect of late twentieth century medical and surgical practice is that patients can neglect their own health responsibilities in the mistaken belief that medical science will rescue them from a life of pain or self-neglect.

If we seek to connect medicine with health, the challenge will become one not only of knowing how to intervene and treat pathology but also how to respect people with low back pain, whose 'right to be' is suffering. Basic to this respect is the patient's 'right to be' informed about spine function, treatment choices, and outcomes.[31]

Education has been increasingly advocated as the primary treatment of low back pain[32] and success demonstrated in back schools.[33] However, a primary care educational model which cares well for people with low back pain has yet to be implemented. It has become clear that this will not be effected until patients and physicians begin to claim their 'right to be.'

Such a respectful low back education approach would avoid expropriating patient power, physician induced disability, and misusing medical care to fix a psychosocial problem. The objective of patient education is for the patient to help himself. This involves becoming informed in decisions regarding his care and claiming a purpose consistent with capacities. But he won't engage in self care behavior until he can hear and value the rhythm of his heart. In order for the physician to be supportive of this, an understanding of the patient's pathology and a coherent concept of health need to be connected. Certain obvious cases of pathology are so severe that the emergency condition would take precedence and override the educational paradigm. But most often the goal is a cooperative blend between the efforts of the patient and the doctor. The challenge for the physician is to know when to intervene in the pathology and when to activate the patient's own capacities. The clinicians of today have many powerful diagnostic and therapeutic resources, making it easy for the physician to aggressively intervene, especially because the discovery of disease is highly compensated. Disability is reinforced by a sys-

Happiness lies in the absorption in some vocation which satisfies the soul.

- William Osler

tem that seems to enable or encourage illness behavior. Holding the tension is difficult for the physician of today because he is steeped long in pathology, but is weak in the knowledge of health education and has little concept of the patient's 'right to be.' This is the challenge of the future, for education is truly the key to the treatment of chronic diseases.

Education as Therapy

The physician is Nature's assistant.

- Galen

Chronic diseases resulting from destructive living patterns have replaced infectious diseases, such as tuberculosis, as today's costly medical concerns and major killers. John Knowles observed that "the next major advance in the health of the American people will come from the assumption of individual responsibility for one's own health and a necessary change in lifestyle for a majority of Americans."[34] The economics of chronic conditions is enormous. These costs may indeed bring on a funding crises[35] because three fourths of U.S. medical care expenditures are directed to the 45 percent of non-institutionalized Americans who have 1 or more chronic conditions.[36] The United States presently leads the world in three medical categories: "Our recovery experience from chronic states is the longest, it is the most expensive, and our population suffering with chronic conditions is increasing at the highest rate."[37] The chronic state is characterized by a sense of vagueness about who we are, what we are doing, and even what day it is.[38] The experience of life begins to slip by in a stream of meaninglessness. Insurer assessment of effective educational programs, such as Page Bailey's Educotherapy, show that the area of greatest improvement is in the level of interest in ways to speed up recovery.[39] Those steps are unique to each individual.

Words are our most powerful medicine, they can heal or they can wound. Physicians' words are known to positively influence health behavior. But as the Institute of Medicine notes "traditional trust is being questioned."[40] Perhaps physicians have become so involved in mastering the technical aspects of managing disease and are now so hassled by the regulatory barriers to caring for people in Federal and managed care practices that they have little energy or time for teaching about healthful behavior. For economic reasons, their good intentions are being diverted from the patient toward complying with the managed-care cost containment regulations.

In medical care, as in the rest of the culture, we are caught in the not so subtle detail of speed and how fast we move. The physician of today is so hurried, harried, and overloaded that there is insufficient time to listen to and empower the patient. This visit, which was traditionally an educational and healing process, has now become a cost effective transaction for the search and treatment of pathology.

Recognizing this problem, Salk in fact did not see the solution coming from medical practitioners and medical schools, and in 1975 called for schools of health.[41] Unfortunately, despite the wisdom of this recommendation over twenty years later there are no schools of health, and the current economic climate of concern about medical costs, makes it unlikely that there will be schools for the education of a totally new health practitioner. The more possible goal will be for physicians to develop respect for the outcomes from health education already being delivered to young people in Asset Development and to adults in Educotherapy. "Health care reform" has thus far proved to be mostly about the economics of managed care. Whether the

Understanding is an emerging experience.

- **Page Bailey**

already overcrowded medical education curriculum will ever teach young doctors to respect health and the 'right to be' will remain to be seen. But on the streets and trails people have always intuitively known they have a right to listen to the "rhythm of their heart." Deep inside there is no doubt; they just don't experience enough collective support for it.

Health Care: An Individual Matter

At the survival level, the fundamental conditions and resources of health are peace, shelter, education, food, income, a stable eco-system, sustainable resources, social justice, and equity.[42] In times of change, health becomes success in response to a challenge or stress, whether it be physiological, psychological or immuno-logical.[43] In health, the patient is the manager and the physician is a resource teacher or partner. The patho-logically based medical model of health (the absence of disease) makes it difficult for physicians to see many "normal" people as healthy. If instead, health is viewed as the capacity to work and to love, we can encourage patients to function despite aging changes, backaches, and degenerative discs.

*There can be
no greater good
than that a man or
beast be given
back his self.*

- R.G.H. Siu

Leon Kass argues that "health is a state of being, not something that can be given. It no more makes sense to claim a right to health, than a right to wisdom or courage . . . To make my health someone else's duty is not only unfair, it imposes a duty impossible to fulfill . . . Doctors and public health officials have only lim-ited powers to improve our health. Health is not a commodity that can be delivered. Medicine can only help those who help themselves."[44] Health resides in the power and action of the individual. Our health is enhanced by the way we choose to live, as well as by public health services, safeguards, and immunizations. Important services are provided by local, state, and federal health departments who monitor air, food, and water quality to guard against communicable and toxic threats.

In 1977, patterns of behavior called lifestyle were estimated to account for 50 percent of mortality from the ten leading causes of death in the United States.[45] Certainly, much HIV-related mortality is lifestyle-related and points again toward the importance of behavior and the need for patient education. Given that health is determined as much by lifestyle and environment as by human biology and medical care,[46] preventive and behavioral medicine can no longer be ignored. Health education, however, still does not command a position of strong respect in 20th century American medicine. Although health and prevention are often linked with treatment, the subject of health is not a part of medical school or textbooks of medicine. The Institute of Medicine report *Medical Education and Societal Needs* discussed infusion of new fields into medical education, including behavioral science, health promotion, and disease prevention. "The major recommendation of this committee was that an Agenda Group on Education of Health Professionals be established."[47] Unfortunately nothing of substance resulted, however the need for health education has not gone away. More recently the Pew Fetzer Report on Health Education and Relationship-Centered Care is attempting to create a health influence for physician education. Their three areas of interest are patient-practitioner relationship, community-practitioner relationship, and practitioner-practitioner relationship.[48] These commendable goals need the focus of the 'right to be' and the tools of speaking, seeing, and relating in a healthy manner.[49]

It is part of the cure to wish to be cured.

- Seneca

We may have more emotional tension or congestion in our lives than we can readily handle.

- Norman Cousins

While general education programs can convey large amounts of information to large numbers of people, there has not yet been a substitute developed for conversing one-on-one with a physician. The moment of greatest potential for turning someone toward health occurs when the patient seeks out a physician. When the complaint is heard, the doctor can determine whether the treatment of choice is education, medication, surgery, or a combination. The title "doctor," in Latin means "teacher: one who gives instruction in some branch of knowledge."[50] A teacher of health is one who has the knowledge, experience, insight, and skill to communicate with compassion to the patient, recognize the essence of her problem, and lead that person in a process of healing. Although medical care and health care are intimately linked and should be played out together in the doctor's office, there is a problem. Neither contemporary practice patterns, managed care regulations, nor utilization reviews allow either time or compensation for physician-patient education. The increasingly technical nature of medical practice and third-party regulation has further carried doctors away from being teachers. The consequence of educational failure is more medical care and increased costs.

Talking with people is a time-intensive activity. Will the physician take the time and necessary resources to do this, or will she quickly write a prescription to dull the patient's discomfort and sense of purpose? If we only operate or medicate, when in reality the treatment of choice calls for education, we take away the patient's power, deny his 'right to be' and perhaps his health potential. The medical world is faced with increasing evidence that education can result in improved patient care while decreasing costs. The key step in meeting the demands of this changing focus, will be to educate physicians to respect the patient's 'right to be.'

The Contemporary American Health Model

The American health model of the past twenty years has been shaped by the two great medical problems of heart disease and cancer. Americans are exposed to information correlating lifestyle with the development of cardiac disease and lung cancer. A low-fat diet, weight and blood pressure control, and not smoking are all advocated by the medical community, based on extensive research data.[51] The benefits of regular exercise,[52] moderation in the use of alcohol,[53] and dangers of substance abuse[54] are also extensively reported. These lifestyle principles constitute responsible self-care today. There is not yet much medical acknowledgment that the heart seeks to align with work satisfaction or may risk a Monday morning heart attack. But there are those such as Marsha Sinetar who know and write that occupational success is tied to healthy human development and that its seminal demand is spiritual growth—the cultivation of those inner gifts and forces that renew and animate our creative energies.[55]

I hadn't yet developed the professional armor that shields us from unanswered questions.

- Richard Sandor, M.D.

But for some specific disorders, education has become a successful component of medical management. Better informed patients are more responsible and make decisions more appropriate to their individual needs. Greenfield and Kaplan, of the New England Medical Center Health Institute, have reported the benefits of patient education prior to physician appointments and measured positive effects in the health of patients with peptic ulcer disease, hypertension, diabetes, rheumatoid arthritis, and breast can-

*Most people think that
medical care is good for
you. The fact is that
some medical care is
good for you, a great
deal is irrelevant and,
unfortunately, some
of it is harmful.*

- **Lester Breslow**

*If you have more
surgeons, you'll get
more surgery. If you
have more internists,
you'll get more
lab tests.*

- **John Wennberg**

cer.[56] Cost savings of between $1.7 million and $3.4 million resulted from an educational program at L.A. County Medical Center, where Miller and Goldstein reported a 50 percent reduction of diabetic patient admissions with a program emphasizing education.[57] Lorig and Holman report that patients in the Arthritis Self-Management Program showed a 19 percent reduction in pain and 43 percent reduction in physician visits after four years. The project showed that if 1 percent of Americans suffering from rheumatoid arthritis and osteoarthritis achieved the same benefits as did the participants in its four-year-follow up, the reduction in medical costs would be $2.9 million and $14.5 million dollars respectively.[58]

The Federal Government provided another important perspective when the United States Public Health Service published Healthy People 2000, a concept of the health future of this country—332 objectives in 22 broad categories, calling on medical and health professionals to prevent, not just to treat, the diseases and conditions that result in premature death and chronic disability."[59] Another program, called The Health of the Public, is working with seventeen medical schools and challenging academic centers to re-evaluate their mission. They, too, have published health-oriented goals and objectives, acknowledging this to be an ambitious task, but noting "the forces for change, especially those external to the academic health center, are powerful and not likely to diminish in the foreseeable future."[60] Fortunately, positive reports have been forthcoming from innovative problem-based medical school curriculum programs, which may bode well for the potential to introduce the concept of health in addition to the treatment of pathology to all medical students.[61]

Salk not only advocated schools of health, he saw a much larger picture, and pointed out that we are now entering an era in which we will choose a path toward health and the development of maximal "self-expression and self-restraint," or choose the "alternative path of limitless license" which will unleash disease, destruction, and pathological greed. Wisdom will be required for survival. Man has a choice to cooperate with nature's process or not. "It does not take too much wisdom to predict who will be favored since nature, and not men, will in effect have the last word." The difference will be "between a philosophy or attitude described by the word *'or,'* for the past [man or nature] and the word *'and,'* for the future"—man and nature.

Salk observes, "The attitude that man is, by definition, born with diseases and that his life must consist, in part, in reducing the negative, is primarily a 'disease-oriented attitude.' The alternative attitude— that maldevelopment and malfunction of biological systems can lead to disease—assumes the existence, of a 'natural' state of health which is subject to dysfunction as a result of post-natal influences."[62]

Health cannot be separated from nature and life's relationships. This is the traditional view of health. Health education can succeed in its blend with technology and intervention. But health encompasses more than teaching self medical care. Health demands an awe for the mystery, as well as understanding of self, community, and nature.

Both ancient and modern physicians function within the archetypal domain of "magic" and mystery—being people whose special knowledge, skills, and tools are used to effect magical and miraculous cures and treat-

The old Lakota was wise. He knew that man's heart away from nature becomes hard.

- Standing Bear, Lakota Sioux

*Man does have a choice,
either cooperate with
the process or not.*

- Jonas Salk

*..psychosomatic
medicine seeks to
preserve the ego; sacred
medicine sought to
free man from
self-illusion and its
psychogical
consequences.*

- Jacob Needleman

ments. Human beings can use these archetypal magician potentials in the service of healing and community. When we do, the deconstructive and sociopathic energies of the immature (dysfunctional magician) are transformed into a mature approach that heals both self and the larger community.[63] The organization of oneself and a community to this end has been the traditional task of the healer.

The archetypal healer pays attention to what has heart and meaning. Healers recognize joy and love are the most potent healing forces available to other humans. Effective healers are characterized by extending love in: acknowledgment, acceptance, recognition, validation, and gratitude.[64]

A traditional healer affirms one's 'right to be a part of the whole.' "People the world over consistently acknowledge each other in one of four ways: We acknowledge each other's skills; each other's character qualities; each other's appearance; or the impact we make on each other. Wherever we receive the least acknowledgment is where we may carry a belief of inadequacy or low self esteem."[65]

Many traditional cultures believe the heart is the bridge between Father Sky and Mother Earth. The four chambered heart of traditional healers is the source for sustaining emotional and spiritual health. They describe this heart as being full, open, clear, and strong. They check daily, asking: "Am I full-hearted, open-hearted, clear-hearted, and strong-hearted? . . . Where we are not full-hearted, we approach people and situations half-heartedly."[66] When my heart is not in my work, life becomes tentative.

When we are not open-hearted, we are becoming closed-hearted. Life is defensive and characterized by meeting resistance and needing to protect ourselves from the possibility of being hurt. When we are not clear-hearted life is filled with confusion and doubt. When we are not strong-hearted there is not enough courage to speak or live our truth. "Courage" from the French word for heart, *coeur,* means "the ability to stand by one's heart or to stand by one's core." When we have courage, we demonstrate the healing power of paying attention to what has heart and meaning for us.[67]

Jeanne Achterberg has characterized a balanced view of healing:
> Healing is a life long journey toward wholeness.
> Healing is remembering what has been forgotten about connection and unity and interdependence among all things living and non-living.
> Healing is embracing what is most feared.
> Healing is opening what has been closed, softening what has hardened into obstruction.
> Healing is entering into the transcendent, timeless moment when one experiences the divine.
> Healing is creativity and passion and love.
> Healing is seeking and expressing self in its fullness, its light and shadow, its male and female.
> Healing is learning to trust life.[68]

Healing involves the principle of reciprocity, the ability to equally give and receive through the ability to connect.[69] If we do not maintain a balance between giving and taking, we create a hole in the universe and in our soul. Giving thanks is the sacred act of keeping the cycle intact which has been honored by traditional natives, by patients who visited the Asclepian temple, and people today.

There is a symbiotic relationship between giving and receiving; each implies the other.

- David Cooper

The foundation of health is the 'right to be a part of

the whole.' The foundation of medicine is the diagnosis and treatment of pathology. Integration of these two functions together is the challenge and goal. But the barriers are formidable.

Barriers to Health Education: Expectations

Among the barriers to health education are four sets of expectations, those of the patient, the doctor, the payment administrator (insurance company or health maintenance organization), and the pharmaceutical suppliers. These four sets of expectations should be compatible and cooperative but are potentially confrontive and counterproductive.

Modifying behavior is more easily said than done, and this is the case for physicians as well as patients. Biomedical knowledge has expanded so rapidly over the past eighty years that it has distanced itself from the art and science of health. The ancient medical tradition of advocacy for healthy behavior and living has become neglected. What was the trunk of the tree of medicine, patient education, does not support today's growth of specialized medical and surgical branches. The roots of the tree in health have been forgotten.

Most of academic medicine and most physicians are now more oriented toward new pharmaceuticals and technical procedures than toward teaching balance and healthy living. Medical training is centered around the treatment of disease, not teaching health and the 'right to be.' The major share of grant money for research is allocated to laboratory-based biomedical research,[70] and in many academic medical centers, attention to biomedical research has even displaced the previous emphasis on training doctors.[71]

In the play of life, the body is the costume, the mind writes the script, and the brain, by means of the nervous system, carries out the acts in the play. The play develops the mind and the quality of mind that is developed determines the quality of action that is immediately available to the individual.

- Page Bailey

Twenty-four, including some of our most prestigious, medical schools do not have family practice training programs.[72] There are, thus, mixed signals on the horizon for health education, and in fact the current expectations of patients, physicians, and insurance carriers pose significant barriers.

Patient Expectations — Over this century, many patients seem to have moved away from taking responsibility for their behavior. A possible explanation may be that even before they fall victim to sickness or injury, some Americans lack confidence and belief in their own abilities and judgment. They have lost their 'right to be' or never had it. In overcrowded urban concentrations, they are increasingly subject to job layoffs and economic fluctuations beyond their control. It stands to reason that if urban dwellers lose power and a sense of meaning in their lives, they no longer retain as much of the old-fashioned ethics of self-sufficiency and responsibility; they will tend to assume a more passive attitude regarding their health. But today, because our world has become increasingly complex and specialized, problem-solving power is transferred to experts who must be consulted. There is less of an individual sense of ability to influence one's destiny. Physicians may want to consider when intervention should be balanced with education, if they want to stop contributing to further deterioration of patient capacities and begin instead promoting patient empowerment.

Information Overload — We live in the "information age." Just as our ancestors lived in agricultural or industrial eras, we dwell in a time where our lives are influenced by an enormous flood of information moving around and through us. Information can be either helpful or harmful. Discernment and knowing how

Nothing is more terrible than ignorance in action.

- Goethe

much is enough are fundamental to health. Confusing or excessive information may exacerbate patients' tendencies to transfer responsibility to their physicians. Never in history was more information and knowledge available to more people; never has wisdom been more needed or endangered. The volume of information in the printed and spoken word has been expanded by television and computerization to exceed the capacity of even the most brilliant people to absorb and integrate. The consciousness can hold only a limited amount of information. Television is accompanied by advertising, much of which may misinform. The promise of an instant solution to problems through the purchase of a product is standard marketing.

The implied message is that technology will solve all problems, and foolish ways of living are encouraged. Those without medical insurance especially need sound health education and may be particularly vulnerable to advertised misinformation. Television has become a third parent and is often not a positive "parent," instead teaching foolish, immediate gratification. At the same time, the role of parents in educating their children is decreasing. Male parent teaching began to diminish years ago, with the industrial revolution and, now, female-parent teaching is decreasing with the entry of most women into the working world.

*Always do
one less thing
than you think
you can do.*

- **Bernard Baruch**

The neocortex of the nervous system will seek stimulation as witnessed by the hours and days passed by people looking at the computer screen at large amounts of information, but much of it neither relevant nor wise. Bly points out that the neocortex needs to deeply experience the sensory world of nature to fully mature. He refers to Wordsworth's observation that growth does not go from childhood to adulthood, but from childhood to *nature* to adulthood. The poet believed that without a time in nature a person will be a child all of his life.[73] TV steals the neocortex's time in nature and gives a little useless information in return. The joy of nature never fills out the heart.

The neocortex loves light, insects, water, and other creatures. But when the brain no longer interacts with the earth and nature, plants and animals, but only its own inventions, curiosity diminishes, as does the fire of life. No bonding occurs, no respect develops. Bly believes we are lying to ourselves about the renaissance the computer will bring. He believes it will bring nothing but the neocortex devouring itself.[74] Certainly the computer opens up a new world of information, but how we value ourselves, each other, and the world is the gauge for how well the tool is used.

The computer is neither creative nor destructive. It is a tool of many facets, and exponentially increases access to information and effectiveness. Like the microscope, it opens up access to information at a new level. That level on the Internet may open to the exact answer and information needed. Or the computer may come on line as a distraction which diverts and drains away awareness and focus from healing and wholeness. It is worthy of note that the microscope opened the door to both improved medical care and germ warfare. Similarly the computer can be healthful or destructive depending on our discernment and intention. The choice is ours, not the computer's. Wisdom is the guide. Without wisdom, the journey quickly becomes confusing and dangerous.

Even with computers, valid health information is too often lacking, because the ability to absorb wisdom is impaired when the cognitive overload becomes excessive. With the potential for confusion during informa-

Your mind is your steering wheel. When other people have control over your steering mechanism, you have no way of knowing where they are leading you.

- Torkom Saraydarian

tion overload, there comes an increased need for meaningful, individualized patient-physician communication. But with overload, language loses meaning for many people.

Language guides our nervous system and our behavior. The discourse of traditional people and their healers grew out of experiences and feelings—from interactions with animals, birds, the earth, trees, and water as well as each other. Their sense of coherence and meaning came directly from the sensuous and spiritual information of life.[75] Their language and behavior moved with the rhythm of the heart and the rhythm of the earth. Each word was sacred, imbued with the power it represented.

Our behavior and language now relate more to machines and tools. As a result, it has becomes faster, more mechanical, less friendly, and less meaningful. Information and words have become voluminous, but much of it useless. Meaning becomes a rare occurrence when language requires no real effort of comprehension.[76] Language and life lose their vitality as we are buried by irrelevant information. Information can become knowledge, but it requires the experience of the essence to become wisdom.

One day in the 1970s, I was invited to have tea with the Dali Lama's physician Yoshe Donden. Several other healers, physicians, and therapists were also present. A young psychologist from New York City who was involved in the growing "health food industry" was eager to ask the first question. He described his practice as caring for young children who were either depressed or hyperactive. Because the beverage of choice for these youngsters was soda pop, he wondered if there might not be an herbal drink which

Here lies the great gift of the Spirit; though we may have lost our way, when we come to that realization, we discover the path once again.

- Lauren Artress

would be better for them. This was all meticulously translated to be certain that it was appropriately understood. With the poise and presence of a master teacher and healer Yoshe Donden said, "American children have too many choices."

The psychologist did not realize his question and purpose had been fully comprehended. In complete detail he presented his question again with emphasis on what herbal drink might be best to solve this behavioral dilemma for his patients and their parents. This time with no additional translation the answer came with the authority and power of the Himalayas and the Tibetan plateau, "American children have too many choices!"

Physician Expectations — More medical care does not always result in better health. It can have the opposite effect.[77] Teaching patients has become overshadowed by the powerful diagnostic and therapeutic armamentarium available to the contemporary physician. While this potential has become truly awesome and should be humbling, it seldom is. Rather, the strong, bright people attracted to medicine and surgery, who are skilled and confident enough to master modern medicine and carry out life-saving treatments, may in fact be corrupted by this added power, and fail in their commitment to health. Do medical doctors like too much to hear patients call them experts? The physician may be right in a difficult condition where quick, decisive action and direction are necessary for saving a life. But for day-to-day living, patient decisions and behavior may be more relevant. Meaningless work is a significant problem. Little habits do add up and may be determinant. The astute clinician who knows when to say, "A pill or procedure is not the answer here," can be influential. On the

It is because each clinical decision involves so many judgments of facts and values that medicine in its highest form will continue to remain an art.

- René Dubos

other hand, a patient may be understandably robbed of action or reflection if he is told "there is nothing that can be done." Sometimes the patient's condition is not hopeless, and would benefit greatly from education to improve balance and coping skills.

Insurance Carrier Expectations — The compensation system determines what is performed in medical care. At present physicians do not expect to be paid for educational services. The current insurance structure encourages and rewards the diagnosis and treatment of pathology. For reasons they have never revealed, most medical insurance companies have taken a strong anti-health education posture, although they have enthusiastically embraced the term "health care" for marketing purposes. Except in rare cases health education is not a compensable benefit. "No serious national educational effort will take place until the problem of reimbursement is solved. The present blanket exclusion of preventive services from federal health insurance programs is not responsive to the current state of knowledge."[78] Simultaneously, economic forces are driving primary care medicine into a high patient volume practice pattern and away from a quality focus where time is taken to talk with patients. The few resource dollars available for education are actually decreasing. The suggestion of "paying doctors more for preventing diseases and less for treating them"[79] would result in changed behavior.

The health of the people is really the foundation upon which all their happiness and all their power as a State depend.

- Benjamin Disraeli

Pharmaceuticals: Modern pharmacology has become highly effective and powerful over the past fifty years. Drugs have always had the ability to seduce and addict. Their current potency is enhanced by new levels of refinement and specificity. Seldom are medications withheld when a physician thinks they may be "indicated." Unfortunately, distinction is not always made between those drugs which

From the past, we can learn in part how to *and* how not to *conduct ourselves.*

-Jonas Salk

are curative or life-essential, those which are palliative, and those which may be unnecessary. The unnecessary prescription written as the "ticket out the door" may be a stumbling block to a patient's self-knowledge and health.

Osler counseled, "One of the first duties of the physician is to educate the masses not to take (unnecessary) medicine[80]. . . Imperative drugging—the ordering of medicine in any and every malady is no longer regarded as the chief function of the doctor."[81] But Osler's words of long ago are seldom heard in modern medical practice, an era of medications and marketing, although there have been attempts in this country to be more discriminating with pharmaceuticals. In 1975, Young reported his decision as Chairman of Medicine at Cook County Hospital to restrict house staff prescriptions of psychoactive and analgesic drugs and encourage patient communication. Patient and house staff surveys later revealed no patient dissatisfaction with the policy. However, some of the medical staff expressed frustration, feeling that they had not done anything for the patient. Further discussions with the patients revealed that if anything the doctor had talked with them more than usual, and patient satisfaction was enhanced rather than diminished.[82] Avorn found that an educational program targeted to physicians, nurses, and aides reduced the use of psychoactive drugs in nursing homes without adversely affecting the overall behavior and level of functioning of the residents."[83] When to medicate and when to educate is a challenging question for the medical doctor, because a prescription can be written quickly, while talking and teaching require more time and care.

The Future of Health and Medical Care

Medicine is largely from the competitive model, physicians compete with illness to defeat cancer, infection,

Economists themselves, like most specialists, normally suffer from a kind of metaphysical blindness, assuming that theirs is a science of absolute and invariable truths, without any presuppositions.

- E. F. Schumacher

and polio. We want to win the war on AIDS. Many of
us believed that health would flow naturally from
winning our competition with disease. Attacking the
problem became the dominant paradigm. War can be
an effective approach. War seemed to be the only
strategy against Hitler, and it was effective. We think
in terms of war being the effective strategy, and sometimes it is. We have had wars on hunger, illiteracy,
and poverty to name a few. For most of our lives,
many of us have only lived in a wartime paradigm.
Medically, I have been trained to war against disease
and suffering. I value medical victories over pathology. But we are missing something.

A language and strategy of war has limitations. It
does not work well when we turn it on each other, our
children or ourselves or the earth. Do we know when
not to attack?

*Of all cooperative
enterprises public
health is the most
important and gives
the greatest returns.*

- William J. Mayo

At the outset, we looked at the flawed thinking that
changed the name of medical insurance to health
insurance. This semantic confusion clouded the issue
in several ways. The most important one for our purposes here is that blurring the distinction between
medicine and health implies that health will be
achieved through a defeat the disease strategy. If we
analyze the need correctly and attack at the right
place we will create health. Wrong! Health will not be
achieved through the interchange of words. But
unless you consciously respect the cooperative
processes essential to health, as well as, the benefits
of medical care you may not see the illusion the cultural mindset is following. We see what we expect to
see. The cultural and political nomenclature is looking to medical doctors for new health responsibilities,
but at present physicians are trained to deliver medical care, not health care.

A medical education is intense and rigorous. During their training, all physicians are likely to see a patient in congestive heart failure decompensate as a result of not understanding or adhering to a prescribed no-salt diet. Physicians know that the medical treatment of choice in this condition is not a pill or a procedure, it is to provide information that results in the appropriate behavior. So they ask the nurse to explain it.

The treatment of choice is education. Optimal medical management requires responsible patient compliance. When patients do not understand or cooperate, or when a physician inappropriately usurps the patient's power and duties, there can be adverse consequences. Today, the confusion of the terms medical care and health care signal a further abrogation of patient accountability, especially in that large population of people who bring to their doctor any of the many lifestyle and spiritual disorders, fears, and psycho-social problems which are expressed as aches and pain.

Educational Therapeutics

A commitment to health is more than a search for pathology. For an understanding of health to become part of medical education a course of study in "educational therapeutics" will be needed in the training of physicians.[84] The medical school department of "educational therapeutics" would teach basic development and respect for the patient's 'right to be,' relationship-centered care[85] and community interdependence,[86] guiding the nervous system toward health,[87] self-care skills, coping with patient dependence and barriers, setting limits and boundaries, using communication skills specific to patient learning styles and needs, health belief models

It is up to each individual to claim their own right to be.

- Tu Moonwalker

and learning theory, working with other health providers and multi-disciplinary treatment teams, studying behavioral and preventive medical principles for individuals and populations and the role of meaning, mystery and spiritual beliefs in health. To gain acceptance by faculty and students, such a course would need to be taught by skilled educators with relevant health experience supported by sufficient academic stature, such that patient education achieves a place alongside pharmacology and surgery in the medical school core curriculum. This faculty will of necessity require non-physicians, as well as medical doctors.

"Educational therapeutics" would restore the physician to his previous place as a supporter of health wisdom—aided by current scientific knowledge and discoveries—for the promotion of health as well as the treatment of disease and injury. The learned and intuitive art of medicine would be evaluated and enhanced. "Educational therapeutics" will be essential to future physicians, particularly the primary-care practitioner. Medicine will have to loosen its hold on the single minded quest for mastery and acknowledge the presence of mystery.[88]

*As joy increases,
the purpose of life
appears more and more
clearly.....*

Torkom Saraydarian

In most cultures, the physician/patient relationship is a clearly stated and acknowledged equal partnership in which doctors are teachers. There will need to be a mutual recognition of the relationship between the patient's 'right to be' and her job satisfaction, and that relationship will ultimately be economically beneficial and stabilizing. Payment reform for health educational services will be necessary. "Health care reform" will have validity and meaning for patients only when physicians study "educational therapuetics" as a part of their medical training and can assist patients in a partnership.

Examining the problem of low back pain from an "educational therapeutics" perspective offers an opportunity to model integration of a traditional view of patient capacities with the modern treatment of disease. There is great value in effectively treating pathology. Much intervention relieves back pain and improves function. But intervention alone or inappropriately used may be insufficient to restore a patient to meaningful participation within the community. The challenge is to know how to simultaneously see a patient's pathology and his 'right to be.'

Unfortunately, few people are able to see this way. In exchange for a patient with low back pain giving up his power and usefulness, he is certified as "medically disabled" and rewarded with a pension. This statement is not about those people with an authentic inability to be useful, but it is to question a system that is too quick to buy a person's innate power and dignity rather than bless it. Despite modern understanding of how the spine functions, physicians, engineers, and scientists have been unable to identify and explain the link between the will and the backbone of the patient. Posture says a great deal about the state of our soul, as well as our back. The spine is the barometer of our well being as well as the axis of our support. Healing is a transformation of meaning in life. Healing may be achieved by a bridge to growth, as well as, by the treatment of pathology.

Health is the state about which medicine has nothing to say: Sanctity is the state about which theology has nothing to say.

- W. H. Auden

Principles for the management of pathology are evaluated by controlled clinical trials, while the response of an individual to his essence, speaking of purpose, is singular and unique. It becomes a case of one, the core of a life. But the essence defies the conclusions of prospective randomized, controlled, double-blind research about life purpose. It will never happen that way. Medical algorhythms, insurance regulations and government administration will never confer that dimension of health. Patient empowerment requires that the physician and community want the patient's value and usefulness to be active not disabled. State of the art treatment of low back pain begins with education, except when the pathology justifies that the doctor intervene and take control and responsibility.

Physician guidelines for low back education are an integration of health and medical principles.

Low Back Pain
Physician Guidelines[89]

1. See the patient as a powerful and useful person with a 'right to be.'
2. Education is the link to hold the tension between the patient's responsibilities and pathology.
3. Know when over-riding the patient's power and responsibility with intervention can result in an improved outcome.

Physicians would do well to be cautious about taking away a patient's 'right to be' and responsibility. The power is given to the patient and he will do with it as he chooses. If you don't claim it, you give it away. Teaching patients about how to care for their backs is not enough. Empowerment of the patient requires support from the community. The education of employers, insurance carriers, and political policy makers who influence the psycho-social factors that promote and encourage illness behavior and disability will also be required. A community or employer who affirm a patient's 'right to be' empowers that person. Optimal treatment is not focused only on the patient's spine pathology but also on the participation of the patient within the community.

Intelligence is the level of operational capacity that is addressed to a specific issue.

- Page Bailey

Life is the sum of all your choices.

- Albert Camus

This will require the ability to hold tension and paradox. This approach is unfamiliar to medical doctors and understandably so because there has been no preparation or training for such action as holding the tension of confusion. The situation may seem overwhelming. But building connections between different worlds, living with confusion, paradox, and holding tension are all part of the work of traditional healers.

The Healing Classroom

Only in Educotherapy do I see the patient in a group setting consistently viewed as a powerful and useful person with a 'right to be.' The remarkable thing about this program has been its success with a wide variety of disorders in addition to low back pain.

There is a famous story about Yoshe Donden when he was invited to make rounds at a major U.S. teaching hospital with physicians and students. At the bedside of one woman, the Tibetan physician held the patient's hand and felt her pulse. He did not speak, but the woman seemed to have received something helpful from him, for she requested that he return again. When they left her room, his hosts inquired what he thought was the cause of her trouble. Yoshe Donden said, "There is a cold wind blowing through her heart that is stealing that woman's strength." The physicians were impressed at his diagnostic understanding and words, for they knew that the woman had a hole in the wall of her heart, a septal defect. Her blood did not circulate normally into her body with each contraction of her heart muscle, but it spilled uselessly between the chambers. Without modern diagnostic technology, Yoshe Donden had arrived at an understanding of the

A joyless person resembles a soulless person.

- Torkom Saraydarian

woman's condition, although he talked poetically rather than in medical language.

What was significant, however, was not appreciated by the other physicians, although I think Dr. MacDonald would have understood. The significance of the story is that when a physician can hear the rhythm of his own heart, when he knows his 'right to be,' he can extend the 'right to be' to a patient and understand the rhythm of her heart. What was significant to the woman was not whether Dr. Donden could speak English, but rather that he could extend to her the 'right to be.' Even with a congenital cardiac defect she could receive that and claim it.

However, even with extensive training, a physician cannot give you the 'right to be.' You must listen to the rhythm of your heart and you must claim it. Play with it when you can. Pay attention to your breathing when you cannot feel the rhythm of your heart. Don't get unnecessarily upset or engaged with frustrations. That is the way it is. Fighting it in many cases is neither effective nor fun. Continuously engaging with conflict is a frustrating and difficult life path. If you elect to listen to the rhythm of your heart and are joined by others, the imbalances will correct. What is difficult for one becomes easier for many. Step out of the way of trouble, taking your essence and your 'right to be' with you. Connect the rhythm of your heart with the rhythm of the earth. Dance and play with joy in the abundance that is given. Become still, and give thanks. Your power resides in your wholeness and purpose. Claim it with reverence for yourself and all of life. Give gratitude to the Creator and all your relationships to keep the cycle flowing.

Where you observe a problem, witness it, take note,

every specialist, whatever his profession, skill or business may be, can improve his performance by broadening his base.

- Wilder Penfield

stay neutral and aware. Notice it and decide whether you will engage or not. Don't become distracted and entangled with every dilemma.

It is helpful to recall how playfully Salk dealt with me when I last talked with him about schools of health. I said, "Some people at the medical school believe they already are a school of health." Salk did not engage with any interest in that argument, he smiled and quipped, "You can't make a cat out of a dog." He did not contest or debate the issue. He was not taken in by the illusion which remained invisible to these doctors. He playfully turned the issue end for end with a simple statement. In other words, recognize medicine is a powerful and valuable service for treating disease, but don't confuse it with health.[90] Health is able to hold the mystery of the unknown with awe.

Rachel Naomi Remen asks the question, "What does it mean to a physician to practice medicine without mystery?" and tells of when she was a medical student. Her school had a large, black tie retirement dinner for a very famous member of the medical faculty, whose scientific contribution had earned him a Nobel prize. This professor was eighty years old and the entire school gathered to honor him. Other famous medical people came from all over the world. The doctor gave a speech describing the progress of scientific knowledge during the fifty years he had been a physician and received a standing ovation.

After the audience had sat down, he remained at the podium and after a brief silence said, "There's something else important that I want to say. And I especially want to tell the students. I have been a physician for fifty years, and I don't know anything more about life now than I did at the beginning. I am no

The physician should speak of that which is invisible. What is visible should belong to his knowledge, and he should recognize the illnesses, just as everybody else, who is not a physician, can recognize them by their symptoms. But this is far from making him a physician only when he knows that which is unnamed, invisible and immaterial, yet efficacious.

- Paracelsus

wiser. It slipped through my fingers." The audience was stunned into silence. Remen reports that in retrospect she realized the remarkable thing he did. "He took an opportunity to warn us about the cage of ideas and roles and self-expectations that was closing around us, even as he spoke to us—the cage that would keep us from achieving our good purpose, which is healing. Healing is a matter of wisdom, not of scientific knowledge."

"We need to heal the wound inflicted on us and on our culture by Descartes'—mind-body split. But this wound goes much deeper; it's also a split between the sacred and the secular."[91]

The great glory of modern medicine is that it regards nothing as essential but the truth.

- Burton J. Hendrick

Education and communication are the two beams on which a bridge can be built linking traditional wisdom with modern technology. The traditional educational connection does not rest on economic profit, but rather rests on "reverence for life" and your 'right to be.' Native people who bless the individual's 'right to be' seem to have a much lower hospitalization rate for low back pain than average Americans. On informal evaluation more than one southwestern group of native peoples show a fraction of the in-patient hospital rates for low back pain compared to the averages from the National Hospital Discharge Summary.[92] Certainly modern American medical care has not reduced the prevalence of low back disability. And the problem does not come from the quality of pathology care, but rather that the best of that kind of care is only partial. As the state of the patient's spine is important, so is the status of his essence, work satisfaction, and community. Medical care is a slice of the pie not the whole.

A step toward the whole is a step toward the integration of education with therapeutic technology, a sacred integration of wisdom. Unnecessary numbers of people live lives that are empty. This emptiness is caused, at least in part, from living without meaning and purpose. The challenge is to recognize that we are always on sacred ground. There is no split between the sacred and the mundane, there is no task that is not sacred in nature and no relationship that is not sacred. "Life is a spiritual practice. Health care, which serves life, is a spiritual practice."[93]

Communication is the other beam of the bridge linking the wisdom of the traditional with the modern. This is horizontal communication between people with mutual respect for diverse gifts and talents. The traditional healer functions as a part of a circle of elders in a community and listens to input from a variety of perspectives. This communication and interaction contrasts with our modern advertising, news, planning committees, political procedures, and corporate boardrooms. Discussions in these busy settings are competitive where influence is achieved by the forcefulness of the orator, the brilliance of the reasoning, or the smooth and honeyed words mouthed to fulfill an expectation or want. "Health care reform" has been such a process conducted within the realm of corporate, professional, and legislative maneuvering. One well known U.S. Senator, discussing Federal Regulation of HMO (Health Maintenance Organization) and Managed Care companies observed, "In too many cases the priority has become higher profits, not better health."[94] Traditional communication is a cooperative circle of trust which holds the value of altruism, that which is best for all concerned. Each person is given time and a respectful audience in which to speak their truth.

For the ancient learning tells us that what may be difficult for one may be easily accomplished by many.

- An Oral History as told by Paula Underwood

The Sacredness and Wholeness of Health

Prayer and a call for spiritual guidance may be a part of either setting, and both are inherent in traditional council. The community of the traditional healer is inclusive rather than exclusive. Only when a person threatens the 'right to be' of a another in the community is exclusionary action taken. If after council that person persists with a threatening posture they are directed to leave. In day to day life traditional healers act as connectors between the various facets of the individual, the community, and the cosmos. Part of their function is to help keep things together.

The traditional healer holds the tension between the sacred and mundane, the conscious and unconscious, and the visible and invisible with exquisite balance. The traditional healer is trained to maintain balance and neutrality. "It is not a balance achieved by synthesis, nor a static condition achieved by resolving opposites. It is not a compromise."[95] Rather, it is a state of acute tension when forces encounter each other, meeting headlong and are not reconciled, but held teetering on the verge of chaos. It is a position with which western thought is uncomfortable. It is an integration of mind and body, patient and community, nature and technology, which we do not vision or hold.

Our focus on pathology prevents us from seeing the whole person, the whole community and the place we have been given in the whole of creation. Specialization separates and divides, making it difficult to embrace the whole. To acknowledge that the whole involves the sacred is unscientific. A physician, who believes and states that the whole might encompass the sacred is chancing career suicide. "If you want to ruin your chance to move up the academic

The flow of energy through a system acts to organize that system.

- Harold Morowitz

Life is a dance of opposites that involves destruction, rebirth, pain, and joy.

- David Fideler

ladder then focus your research on the clinical roles of spirituality and religious commitment," says Dr. David Larson a Maryland psychiatrist and epidemiologist.[96] The traditional healer is at home with the sacred as well as disease. Reclaiming the sacred requires the ability to see the objective and subjective world simultaneously.[97]

Recalling the mysterious and wonderful experience I had as a child of feeling blessed by my pediatrician, Dr. MacDonald, I wondered how many medical students today have had that experience. I took the time to find out at my annual lecture on the "spine and clinical correlations" for the freshman anatomy class.

I asked the students, "How many of you had a positive experience with the family doctor or pediatrician who cared for you as you grew up? About thirty students raised their hands and I was encouraged, I went further. I related my positive experience as a child with Dr. MacDonald and asked, "How many of you felt affirmed by your doctor as you grew up?" No one raised their hand it was not a concept which fit with their world view or experience. I asked, "How many of you have had a negative experience with a doctor?" Again about thirty students out of 130 held up their hands.

Lastly I asked, "How many of you have been shamed by a doctor?" I was surprised by the number and after my lecture asked the anatomy professor how many students had been shamed by the first week of their medical education. He said, "Over half the class."

The reason for all of this shaming in our medical educational system is to teach technical competence. In an effort to train physicians competent in the power-

Joy is a special wisdom.

- Torkom Saraydarian

Before me it is blessed, above me it is blessed Before me it is blessed, above me it is blessed All around me it is blessed My speech is blessed

- The Blessingway

ful skills of today, there is instilled a sense in students that you must perform with perfection, for a patient's life will depend upon it. Just as no one would not want to fly in an airplane with a pilot who forgot to put the wheels down, no one wants to trust their life with an incompetent doctor. The teaching of today is shame-based in an effort to achieve a high standard of competence. The teaching of tomorrow should aspire to a higher standard: competence and the ability to affirm the 'right to be'. People like to fly on airlines where the pilot makes safe and smooth take offs and landings, and talks to them from the cockpit in a calm voice that is reassuring and affirming. The highest goal for physician training should be to teach both technical competence and the benevolence inherent in the 'right to be.' Right behavior calls for this.

That person will never understand himself or herself until he or she has consciously loved the pond and the meadow.

- Robert Bly

Educational systems seek to teach the right behavior to young people. When someone's life is in your hands the stakes are very high, as is the case with the training of physicians and surgeons. Abram tells of how the Apache guide right behavior in their young people. Teaching stories are linked with places in the local landscape. Geographical place names have potent and dynamic meanings that are actively rooted in events which become teaching stories regularly recounted throughout the community. These tales are related by aunts, uncles, parents, and grandparents to guide right behavior. The land and elders are ever vigilant guardians of right behavior for the Apache culture. A story always begins and ends with the geographical place name where the event occurred.

When an Apache person offends the community by a certain action, an elder will recount an appropriate story. Although the offender is not identified or named, they will know if the tale is on target and will feel its effect. The story will begin to work on her, making her want to change her ways and "live right." For she will continually encounter that place in the land where it all happened. The place will keep "stalking her."[98]

This Apache teaching and guidance toward right behavior takes place within a culture built on the 'right to be' of each individual. It is a culture where the backbone of the medical system is the "Blessingway." Without the 'right to be,' messages of shame such as "You can't sing" may silence the voice of a young soprano for years, or a even lifetime. Statements such as "That picture is trash, you can't paint," can kill the talent of a young artist. Shaming will make it more difficult for people to develop their talents and share them with the community. It becomes more difficult to believe we have gifts and talents when no one else believes in them. In traditional healing, loss of those parts of ourselves is called "soul loss." Severe shaming is sufficient to cause such self displacement and can have catastrophic effects on health, identity, and productivity. It would be wonderful if everyone were resilient enough to shrug off these shamings, but often we can't.[99]

Many times without the 'right to be' the wound becomes a disability. He gives up and no longer fights to keep the flame burning. The empty disabled shell still moves, but doesn't contribute much. "Soul loss" is seen by traditional healers as the gravest diagnosis and cause of illness and disease. Yet it is never mentioned at all in modern western medical books or training.[100]

Everyone's motivation is, of course, to educate excellent doctors who help patients to stay well and func-

When the sense of responsibility dulls, the downfall of an individual or a nation begins.

- Torkom Saraydarian

When there is fear the bird of joy flies away.

- Torkom Saraydarian

*There are two desires
natural in man, one of
food for the sake of the
body, and one of
wisdom for the sake
of the diviner
part of us....*

- Plato, Timaeus

*In my experience, the
more true we are to
our creative gifts the
less there is any outer
reassurance or help
at the beginning.*

- David Whyte

tional. The most effective teacher is the one who inspires through behavior and enthusiasm for what she loves, her work and purpose. "If you teach people with joy, they will understand your teaching, and they will try to live according to your teaching."[101]

At present, shaming is inevitable in our culture. When someone attacks and seeks to put shame on you, step out of the way. As you move take all of your parts with you. Say "I don't want to be shamed today." Shame is an oppressive heavy load that smothers the light within you. It is much lighter to carry your essence and 'right to be.' Allow your essence to connect with the Creator and His plan. Some people may not be happy when you no longer allow them to shame you. They may become angry and confused by your change. That's all right. Extend to them the 'right to be' angry and confused, but hold fast with reverence to the joy in the rhythm of your heart. The healing of the medical system and the healing of the world will happen one heart at a time.[102] Keep your wholeness, don't withdraw and contract into fear. Continue to extend love and healing energy in the presence of all life. Anytime I do not believe that I, my children, and all forms of life have the 'right to be,' I become an endangered species. Without a 'right to be' we are like a tree without roots.

Medical care will either choose to evolve, in affirming the 'right to be,' concurrently with developing its technology, or medicine will remain focused only on the pursuit and treatment of disease. Forcing self responsibility onto people without affirming the rhythm of their heart will become an increasingly uncomfortable fit. Recognize that not all will seek to claim their 'right to be.' Not all will want to claim their purpose.

You cannot give what you have not received. Those who have come through the fire of a shame-based education but who have never been blessed have difficulty understanding this. Some will analyze the situation and determine that the 'right to be' should never be part of healing. They will search diligently for more pathology, but will never believe without scientific proof. When discussing this dilemma Ken Wilber points out that you can master systems theory without necessarily going through the transformation of developing postformal awareness.[103] A physician can master the understanding and treatment of pathology, but he will not be able to affirm a patient's 'right to be' if he has never experienced his own. Committing to this path is at present difficult for institutions and medical journals. Much of future medical research will continue "as usual." To paraphrase Wilber, the puzzle of the 'right to be' will not be grasped without experience on the part of participant-observers. The deepest of scientific taboos, the sanctity of the detached observer and prospective controlled study does not insure competence in extending the 'right to be.' It insures failure to grasp the process at the very start. You cannot make a man whole, with meaningful purpose, through an analytical research study. Research can show that those individuals with a meaningful purpose do seem to live longer. Studies at Duke University from 1955 to 1979 demonstrated that out of multiple physical, mental, and social factors human longevity correlated most strongly with work satisfaction.[104] Volunteers aged 60 to 94 demonstrated the number one way to longevity was to maintain a useful and satisfying role in society.[105] However each expression of usefulness is unique.

As with any skill, all are wisely invited down the path. Yet none are encouraged past their own interest, none

You can only hear what your belief allows you to hear.

- Page Bailey

In the middle of the road of my life I awoke in a dark wood where the true way was wholly lost.

- Dante

are encouraged past the edges of their own purpose.[106] Children and adults grow as they choose and as they are able. Senge writes the same message in regard to the "learning organization," warning that any path of growth is a matter of personal choice. Corporations and organizations can get into deep difficulty if they become too aggressive in promoting growth for their members. Overzealous managers who have failed to respect people's personal boundaries or religious beliefs have incurred legal actions against organizations. Senge councils that to support the growth of "personal mastery" (which encompasses much of the 'right to be') leaders and organizations can be most helpful when they foster a climate in which these principles are modeled and practiced in daily life.[107] What we do speaks more loudly than our words.

If I am not for myself, who will be?

- Pirke Arot

The process of healing is one of growth; learning to actively live with what is. Disease is stagnation. Growth is marked by transition periods of confusion and questioning. Information is power. But it takes wisdom to guide that power. The two lions that guard the gates of Eastern temples are said to represent confusion and paradox; the practitioner who would have true wisdom must be willing to pass through both.[108]

You can experience it in visiting mountains and oceans, but you can make better contact with joy by observing the night skies with the millions of stars.

- Torkom Saraydarian

For traditional healers, the mysteries of nature have always been the manifestation and the doorway to healing and there has been both inherent awe and sacredness in this relationship. The power and harmony of our connection to nature is fundamental to wholeness and a viable path to health.

Deep snow surrounds the hut. All around is stillness. Some of the snow crystals are illuminated by the sunlight. They burn like bright stars on the expanse of white drifts. Nothing is moving in the cold clear morning air.

My light is calm and steady, moving with the rhythm of the earth. The snow is melting and the waters in the Crystal and Roaring Fork rivers are rising. There are now bluebirds hopping on the rocks and flying over the river where ouzel dances. Spring and new life are rising from the earth and in my heart. Renewed joy is flowing in the cycle of universal energy.

> May beauty and blessings be before me
> May beauty and blessings be beside me
> May beauty and blessings be behind me
> May beauty and blessings be above me
> May beauty and blessings be beneath me
> May beauty and blessings be within me

For my children's children for seven generations to come, I see health, but not in a book, a building, a new lab test, or pill. It will happen as parents and grandparents touch the land with respect, and experience joy coming into their roots.

When that occurs they will go back into their homes, unplug the computer, TV, and video game and say, "Come outside."

Those who listen in the meadows, on the ridges, by the streams and in their gardens or sacred spaces will hear the rhythm of their heart and feel the rhythm of the earth around them. Allow that energy to heal, recharge and support you, as you claim your 'right to be.'

The union of the self with Nature is integral to the life of tranquility.

- R.G.H. Siu

Resources

Walking with Respect

The World Wide Labyrinth Project
    Veriditas
    Grace Cathedral
    1100 California Street
    San Francisco, California 94108
    (415) 749-6356

Speaking with Respect

    Dialogos, Inc.
    11B Jolly Way
    Scotts Valley, California 95066
    (408) 438-8350

    Boulder Learning Series
    2370 Point of Pines
    Boulder, Colorado 80304
    (303) 417-1125

Seeing with Respect

    Search Institute
    Suite 210
    700 S. Third Street
    Minneapolis, Minnesota 55415
    (612) 376-8955
    (800) 888-7828

    Page Bailey Institute for
    the Recovery Sciences
    P.O. Box 580
    Carbondale, Colorado 81623
    (970) 963-1751
    (800) 460-7339
    6506 S. E. Reed College Place
    Portland, Oregon 97202
    (503) 775-7668

Integrating Health in Community with Respect

Health Resilience Paradigm
415 East Hyman Ave.
Suite 301
Aspen, Colorado 81611
(970) 925-4149

References

Introduction

[1] Weatherford, Jack. *Indian Givers,* Fawcett Columbine, New York, 1988 135.

[2] Burton, Bruce. Iroguois Confederate Law and the Origins of the U. S. Constitution, *Northeast Indian Quartery,* Fall 1986, 4-9.

[3] Weatherford, *Indian Givers,* 135-7.

[4] *Ibid.* 149.

[5] Vogel, Virgil. *American Indian Medicine,* Ballantine Books, New York, 1970, 1, 79,80.

[6] Schaef, Anne Wilson, *Native Wisdom for White Minds,* One World Ballantine Books, New York, 1995, November 4 Entry.

[7] Tresolini, CP and the Pew-Fetzer Task Force, *Health Professions Education and Relationship-centered Care.* San Francisco, CA: Pew Health Professions Commision, 1994, 15.

[8] Mark 12: 28-34.

[9] This terminology is attributed to Page Bailey in relation the psycho-social status of a patient we both treated who suffered with a repetetive motion disorder.

[10] Goffman Catherine, Rice Dorthy, Sung Hai-Yen. Persons with Chronic Conditions. *JAMA,* 1996; 276. 18: 1473-9.

[11] Salk, Jonas. *The Survival of the Wisest,* Harper and Row, New York, 1973, 101.

[12] Hyman, Sidney. *Aspen Idea,* Univ. of Oklahoma Press, Norman, Oklahoma 1975, 81.

[13] Schweitzer, Albert. *The Philosophy of Civilization,* The Macmillan Company, New York, 1960, preface xv.

[14] Andersen, Paul. Aspen needs another Albert Schweitzer. Aspen Times, December 5, 1996, 7.

[15] Hyman, Sidney. *Aspen Idea*, 84.

[16] Schweitzer, Albert. *The Philosophy of Civilization,* 209.

[17] Leonard, George, *The Silent Pulse,* E. P. Dutton, New York, 1978, 135.

[18] Schweitzer, Albert. *Civilzation and Ethics,* Macmillan Co, New York, 1960, preface 84.

Chapter One

[1] Sharif Abdullah, *Yes! A Journal of Positive Futures,* Bainbridge Island,Washington, Beta Issue, #B2, 28.

[2] Cameron, Julia. *The Vein of Gold.* Tarcher/Putnam, New York,1996, 34.

[1] Kass, Leon. *Toward a More Natural Science,* The Free Press, New York, 1985,170

[2] This definition contains my emphasis on the cooperative aspects of health, but with acknowledgement to Aaron Antonovsky for his insightful definition of health cited in the introduction.

[3] Cowen, Elliot. *Plant Spirit Medicine,* Swan Raven and Co. Newberg, Oregon, 1995, 30.

[4] I am indebted to Chuck Little for his observations regarding wholeness in our conversations.

[5] Boldt, Laurence G. *Zen and the Art of Making a Living,* Penguin Group, New York, 1991, 1992, 1993, prologue, xi

[6] Bailey, Page. Educotherapy, Basic 300 Teachings, #60.

[7] Boldt, Laurence. *Zen and the Art of Making a Living,* xi.

[8] Bailey, Page. Basic 300 Teachings, #198.

[9] Jung, Carl. *Memories Dreams and Reflections.* Vintage Books, New York, 1961, 1962, 1963,340.

[10] Bailey, Page. Basic 300 Teachings, #295.

[11] Schaef, Anne Wilson. *Native Wisdom for White Minds.* Oct. 25 Entry.

[12] Saraydarian Torkom, *Joy and Healing,* The Aquarian Educational Group, Sedona, Arizona, 1987; 1.

[13] Report of a Special Task Force to the Secretary of Health, Education and Welfare. *Work in America.* MIT Press, Cambridge, Mass. 1973, 79.

[14] Bailey, Page.

[15] Hendricks, Gay. New Dimensions Radio Interview. February 1997.

[16] Bigos S, Spengler D *et al.* Back Injuries in Industry: a retrospective study. III. Employee related factor, *Spine* 11:252, 1986.

[16] Battie M, Bigos S *et al.* A prospective study of the role of cardiovascular risk factors and fitness in industrial back pain complaints, *Spine* 14:141, 1989.

[17] Dossey, Larry. *Meaning and Medicine,* Bantam, New York, 1991, 12. This book by Larry Dossey on the role of meaning in health and illness is essential reading for understanding the power of this concept in disease. This is the text book for the Educotherapy Recovery Curriculum.

[18] Senge, Peter. *The Fifth Discipline,* Doubleday, New York, 1990; 171.

[19] Sardello, Robert. *Work and the Soul,* Lapis, 55.

[20] Rathbun, Robin. *The Search for Soulful Work,* Nexus. March April 1997, 23-4.

[21] Boldt, Laurence. *Zen and the Art of Making a Living,* xii,xiii.

[22] Houston, Jean. Calling Our Spirits Home. *Noetic Sciences Review.* Winter 1994, 5-11.

[23] Gretchen Swan has called to my attention that a seed is destroyed in the germination process. It cannot do both, remain a seed and also become a plant or tree.

[24] Schweitzer, Albert. *Reverence for Life,* Fulfill your destiny, Translated by Reginald Fuller, Irvington Publishers, Inc. New York, 141.

[25] *Ibid,* 117.

[26] I am grateful to Edgel Pyles for his teaching about shame. He brought understanding to the meaning and significance of shame in my own healing. From this awareness can grow the importance of how we live and teach our children. The desire to bless and be blessed becomes a way of life.

[27] Bailey, Page. Basic 300 Teachings #271.

[28] Borysenko, Joan, *Guilt is the teacher love is the lesson.* Warner, New York, 1990.

[29] Bailey, Page. Teaching in Glenwood Springs Educotherapy Class. 1996.

[30] Bradshaw, John. *On: The Family,* Health Communications, Inc. Deerfield Beach, Florida,1988, 2.

[31] Page Bailey, Recovering Class Glenwood Springs, Colorado, March 24, 1997.

[32] Erickson, Erik, *Childhood and Society,* Second Edition. W.W. Norton, New York, 1950, 1963, 247-51.

[33] Personal Communication from Marilyn Youngbird, August 3, 1994. She was appointed Indian Commisioner of Colorado by Governor Richard Lamm.

[34] Speech made by Jonas Salk at the Limits to Medicine Congress, Davos Switzerland, 1975.

[35] Bly, Robert. *The Sybling Society,* Addison-Wesely Publishing Co., Reading, Mass, 1996, 67-88.

[36] Notes from a course taught by Rabbi Zalman Schachter-Shalomi at Naropa shared by Pat Hopkins.

[37] Mather, Kirtley. *The Permissive Universe,* University of New Mexico, Albuquerque, 1986, 188.

[38] Roaring Fork Sunday, December 1-7, 1996, vol 2: issue 4, 1.

[39] From the *Transformational Learning Commmunity* on the Internet. Attributed to Tom Atlee, URL: http://www.trnasform.org/transform/introduction.html I am grateful to Bob Goldhammer for sharing this material with me.

⁴⁰ Mails, Thomas. *The Hopi Survival Kit,* Stewart, Tabori and
   Chang, New York, 1997,195.

⁴¹ Mohler, Stanley *et al. Circadian Rhythms and the Effects of
   Long Distance Flights.* Federal Aviation Administration, l968

⁴² Moore-Ede, Martin *et al, The Clocks that Time Us.* Harvard
   University Press, Cambridge, Mass. 1982, 138.

⁴³ Gander, Philippa. *et al,* Age, *Circadian rhythms, and Sleep
   Loss in Flight Crews.* Aviation, Space and Environmental
   Medicine; 64:3, 189,1993.

⁴⁴ Mohler, Stanley. *Circadian Rhythms and the Effects of Long
   Distance Flights,* Federal Aviation Administration. April,
   1968, AM68-8, 1.

⁴⁵ Walker, Deward E. Jr. Protection of American Indian Sacred
   Geography, Chapter in *Handbook of American Indian
   Religious Freedom.*, edited by Christopher Vecsey, Crossroad,
   New York, 100-15.

⁴⁶ Personal communication from Evan Hodkins regarding a
   comment by Rabbi Zalman Schachter-Shalomi.

⁴⁷ Notes from a course taught by Rabbi Zalman Schachter-
   Shalomi at Naropa Institute in Boulder Colorado provided by
   Pat Hopkins.

⁴⁸ Cousins, Norman. *Head first.* E. P. Dutton, New York, 1989, 25.

⁴⁹ Schweitzer, Albert. *Out of My Life and Thought.* Henry Holt
   and Co., New York, 1933, 1949, 1990, 148-53.

⁵⁰ *Ibid.,* 152.

⁵¹ *Ibid.,* 154,55.

⁵² Cousins, Norman. *Dr. Schweitzer of Lamberene.* Harper and
   Brothers, New York, 1960, 190.

⁵³ Evans, William. A Cross Sectional Prevelance Study of Lumbar
   Disc Degeneration in a Working Population. *Spine,* 14: 1,60-
   4,1989.

⁵⁴ Cameron, Julia. *The Vein of Gold,* 25.

⁵⁵ *Ibid.,* 27.

⁵⁶ Attributed to Paul Dudley White who was physician for
   President Dwight Eisenhower when he suffered a heart
   attack. Cited in *Healthwalk,* Carlson, Bob and Seiden, O.J.
   Fulcrum, Golden, Colorado, 1988.

⁵⁷ Cited in *Meaning and Medicine* by Larry Dossey: Archibald
   MacLeish, quoted in Rollo May, *Paulus; Tillich as Spritual
   Teacher,* (Dallas: Saybrook, 1988,) 118.

⁵⁸ Bailey, Page. Basic teaching of Educotherapy.

⁵⁹ Bohm, David. "Meaning and Information," in *The Search for
   Meaning,* Paavo Pylkkanen, ed., Wellingborough,
   Northamptonshire, England: Crucible, 1989, 51.

⁶⁰ Dossey, Larry. *Meaning and Medicine,*13.

[61] *Ibid.,* 14.

[62] Saraydarian, *Torkom. Joy and Healing,* 8.

[63] *Ibid.,* 9.

[64] *Ibid.,* 10.

[65] Chesterton, GK. *The Defendant.*

[66] This is one of several descripitive terms for our culture of technological creations. Jerry Mander uses these words *In the Absence of the Sacred.*

[67] Dossey, Larry. *Meaning and Medicine,* 12.

[68] Schweitzer, Albert, *Philosophy of Civilization,* 334.

[69] Schweitzer, Albert, *Out of My Life and Thought.* 200

[70] Barnett, Lincoln. *The Universe and Dr. Einstein,* Bantam Books, New York, 1957, 108.

[71] Bailey, Page. Educotherapy, Basic 300 Teachings, #192.

[72] Jung, Carl. *Memories, Dreams and Reflections,* 340.

[73] Kahn, H. *The Path of Initiation,* Servire, Katwijk aan Zee, Netherlands, 1979, 44.

[74] Schweitzer, Albert. *Philosophy of Civilization.* 337.

[75] Schweitzer, Albert. *Out of My Life and Thought,* 157

[76] Artress, Lauren. *Walking a Sacred Path,* Riverhead Books, New York, 1995, 8,9.

[77] Aspen Times, vol. 68 no. 28, July, 1949

[78] Bailey, Page, Educotherapy Basic 300 Teachings #243.

[79] Mander, Jerry. *In the Absence of the Sacred.* Sierra Club Books, San Francisco, 1991, 25-36.

[80] Salk, Jonas, *Survival of the Wisest.* 29.

[81] Schweitzer, Albert. *Philosophy of Civilization,* prface xv.

[82] Schweitzer, Albert. *Philosophy of Civilization,* 283.

[83] Franklin, Benjamin, *Sayings of Poor Richard.* Fleming H. Revell Co. Westwood, New Jersey, 1960, 29.

Chapter Three

[1] In addition to dreams, as well as visions, noted by Jung to be of great significance. Information received in feelings, intuitions, symbols and waking visions are also significant to Tom Brown, who was from his youth trained by Stalking Wolf, a Lipan Apache.

[2] Kharitidi, Olga. *Entering the Circle,* Harper Collins, San Francisco, 1996.

[3] Schweitzer, Albert. *Out of My Life and Thought,* 204.

[4] Schaef, Ann Wilson. *Native Wisdom for White Minds,* July 18.

[5] Ywahoo, Dhyani, *Voices of Our Ancestors,* Shambhala, Boston, 1987, 88.

[6] Bradshaw, John. *Healing the Shame that Binds You.* Health Communications, Deerfield Beach, Florida, 1988; 26.

[7] *Ibid.,* 39.

[8] Maslow, AH. *The Farther Reaches of Human Nature.* Viking Press, New York; 1971, 231.

[9] Roberts, David. *Once They Moved Life the Wind,* Simon and Schuster, New York, 1993; 211.

[10] Somé, Malidoma, *Ritual,* Swan Raven and Company, Portland; 29.

[11] Yawhoo, Dhyani. *Voices of Our Ancestors,* 55.

[12] Romans 1:19

[13] Somé, Malidoma Patrice. *Ritual,* 79.

[14] Edie Swan has been a great help to me in explaining the centrality and significance of blessing to a system of medicine and healing.

[15] Showstack J, Lurie N, Leatherman S, Fisher E, Inui T. Health of the Public, *JAMA,* Oct 2, 1996:276; 13,1071-74.

[16] Press Release January 7, 1997 Community Health Improvement Requires Diverse Partnerships, Careful Monitoring. Institute of Medicine.

[17] Stoto M, Abel C, Dievler A, Editors. *Healthy Communities: New partnerships for the future of public health.* First year report of the Committee on Public Health, Institute of Medicine, National Academy Press, Washington, D.C. 1996,1-5.

[18] Cousins, *Dr. Schweitzer of Lamberene,* 98.

[19] Edie Box, Sr spoke in Glenwood Springs, Colorado on April 23, 1993 on the first return of the Ute people to the Roaring Fork Valley in 100 years.

[20] Proverbs 14:30

[21] Proverbs 17:22

[22] Proverbs 4:23

[23] J. R. Worsley taught me acupunture and Chinese Medicine in Oxford from 1974-1978.

[24] Huang, Chungliang Al and Lynch Jerry. *Mentoring,* Harper Collins, San Francisco, 1995, 25.

[25] Kahn, Hazrat. *The Path of Initiation,* 77.

[26] This Dayak (Borneo) proverb is cited by Carlson, Bob and Seiden, O.J. in *Healthwalk.* Fulcrum, Golden, Colorado 1988, 37.

[27] Schweitzer, *Out of My Life and Thought,* 224-6.

[28] *Ibid.,* 223.

[29] Mander, *In the Absence of the Sacred,* 122.

[30] *Ibid.,* 123.

[31] Jung, Carl. *Memories, Dreams and Reflections,* 340.

[32] Bopp, Judie et al, *The Sacred Tree,* Four Worlds International Institute for Human and Community Development, Lethbridge, Canada, 1984, 20.

[33] Cowan, Eliot. *Plant, Spirit, Medicine,* 106.

[34] Ibid., 106.

[35] Shaw, Mildred. *Schweitzer: Initial Talk,* Aspen Times (Daily Sentinel Staff), July, 1949 vol. 68 no. 28.

[36] Lorler, Maire-Lu.*Shamanic Healing,* 25.

[37] *Ibid.,* 30.

[38] Bopp, Judie. *The Sacred Tree,* 7.

[39] Kahn, Hazrat. *The Path of Initiation,* 35.

[40] Niebuhr, Reinhold. *Moral Man and Immoral Sociey,* Peter Smith Publishers, Magnolia, Mass., 1990.

[41] Ueshiba, Morihei. *The Art of Peace,* Shambhala, Boston, 1992, 100.

[42] Saraydarian, Torkom. *Joy and Healing,* 70.

[43] Artress, Lauren. *Walking a Sacred Path,* Riverhead Books, New York, 1995, 12-3.

[44] *Ibid.,* 33-4.

[45] Kahn, Hazrat. *The Path of Initiation,* 79.

[46] *Ibid.,* 82.

Chapter Four

[1] Duhl, Leonard. *The Social Context of Health in Health for the Whole Person,* Westview Press, Boulder, Colorado; 1980, 45.

[2] Fiedmann, E *et al,* "Animal Companions and One-year Survival of Patients after Discharge from a Coronary Care Unit." *Public Health Rep.* 95;1980, 307-312.
Gunby, P. "Patient Progressing Well? He May Have a Pet," *JAMA* News, 241, 1979,438.

[3] Postlewaite, Maggie. Adaptive gardening tips, *Outreach,* Spalding Rehabilitation Hospital, Spring, 1993 Issue, 9.

[4] Knutson, Andie. *The Individual, Society, and Health Behavior,* Russel Sage Foundation, New York; 305-6.

[5] *Alcoholics Anonymous,* Alcoholics Anonymous World Services, Inc. New York, 1976, 12.

[6] Jung, Carl.*Word and Image,* Princeton Univ. Press, 1979; 125.

[7] Starhawk, Audio Tape.

[8] Matthew 5:14-5.

[9] Somé, Malidoma Patrice, *Ritual,* 67.

[10] *Ibid.,* 67.

[11] *Ibid.,* 67.

[12] *Ibid.,* 67.

[13] *Ibid.,* 68.

[14] *Ibid.,* 69.

[15] *Ibid.,* 69.

[16] Dalai Lama, *My Tibet,* Univ. of California Press, Berkeley, 1990, 139.

[17] Artress, Lauren. Walking the Sacred Path, 72.

[18] *Ibid.,* 21.

[19] *Ibid.,* 23

[20] *Ibid.,* 25.

[21] Ywahoo, Dhyani. *Voices of Our Ancestors,* Shambhala, Boston, 1987; 78, 151.

[22] For an example of Council in Greek culture Zimmerman and Coyle sight *The Anger of Achilles:* Homer's Iliad, Translated by Robert Graves, Doubleday, 1959, 44.

[23] Bohm, David. *On Dialogue,* David Bohm Seminars, Ojai, California, 1990, 1.

[24] *Ibid.,* 2.

[25] Schaef, Anne Wilson. *Native Wisdom for White Minds,* Oct 24th entry.

[26] Zimmerman, Jack and Coyle, Virginia. *Council,* The Ojai, Foundation, 1990, 2.

[27] Jones, Michael. *Yes! a Journal of Positive Futures,* Bainbridge Island, Wash. Beta Issue B2, 40.

[28] Bohm, David *On Dialogue.* 1-41.

[29] Isaacs, William. *Taking Flight: Dialogue, Collective Thinking and Organizational Learning.* pre-publication draft. 27-8.

[30] Senge, Peter. *The Fifth Discipline,* Doubleday, New York, 1990, Introduction, xii,xiii.

[31] Kofman, Fred and Dhority Lynn, *Dialgue,* Leading Learning Communities, Boulder, Colorado, 1995; 5.

[32] *Ibid.,* 7-8.

[33] Zimmerman and Coyle, *Council,* 18-9.

[34] Jones, Michael,*Yes! A Journal of Positive Futures,* Beta Issue, B2,40.

[35] Teaching by Mitch Saunders in St. Marys Hospital Dialogue, Grand Junction, Colorado,1996.

[36] Werner, Emily. *Children of the Garden Island,* Scientific American, April, 1989.

[37] Demos, Virginia. *Resiliency in Infancy,* Chapter in *The Child of Our Times,* ed. Dugan and Coles, Brunner/Mazel, New York,1989, 4.

[38] Bernard, Bonnie. *Fostering Resiliencey in Kids,* Western Regional Center for Drug Free Schools and Communities, Northwest Regional Educational Laboratory, Portland, Oregon, 1991,1.

[39] Werner, Emily. Speech at Prevention Partners Conference, Denver, Colorado, April 9, 1995.

[40] Burns, Timothy. *From Risk to Resilience,* Marco Polo Group, Dallas, 1994, 79, 81.

[41] Benson, Peter *et al. What Kids Need to Succeed,* Free Spirit
Publishing, Minneapolis, 1994.

[42] The Search Institute, 700 S. 3rd St., Minneapolis, MN 55415

[43] Benson, Peter. *Developmental Assets Among Albuquerque
Youth: The Urgency of Promoting Healthy Community,*
Search Institute, 1996, 12-3.

[44] Bailey, Page. *Recovering,* The Page Bailey Institute,
Carbondale, Colorado, 1994.

[45] Saraydarian, Torkom. *Joy and Healing,* 121.

[46] Bailey, Page. Basic 300 Teachings, # 19.

[47] See the Resources section at the back of the book for locations.

[48] Senge, Peter. *The Fifth Discipline,* 7-8.

[49] *Ibid.,* 141.

[50] Ford, Henry. *Detroit News,* February 7, 1926.

[51] Senge, Peter. *The Fifth Discipline,* 139 and 142.

[52] Huang and Lynch, *Mentoring,* 9.

[53] Weatherford, Jack *Indian Givers,* 143.

[54] Wall, Steve and Arden, Harvey. *Wisdom Keepers,* Beyond Words
Publishing, Hillsboro, Oregon, 1990, 7.

[55] *Ibid.,* 33.

[56] *Ibid.,* 16.

[57] *Ibid.,* 63.

[58] *Ibid.,* 68.

[59] *Ibid.,* 75.

[60] *Ibid.,* 97.

[61] *Ibid.,* 120.

[62] Salk, Jonas. *Survival of the wisest,* 109.

[63] *Ibid.,* 116.

[64] *Ibid.,* 110.

Chapter Five

[1] Adapted from a traditional Jewish folk tale *The Physician*
printed by Parabola, New York, vol III:1, 57.

[2] Webster Medical Dictionary, Merriam Webster, Springfield
Mass. 1986, 522.

[3] Leaf, Alexander. Forward in *Stress, Diet and Your Health,* by
Dean Ornish, Holt, Rinehart and Winston, New York,1982,xix-
xxi.

[4] Lorler, Marie-Lu. Shamanic Healing, 81.

[5] *Ibid.,* 34.

[6] Bender, George. *Great Moments in Medicine,* Northwood
Institute Press, Detroit, 1966, 50-5.

[7] *Ibid.,* 56-61.

[8] *The Columbia Encyclopedia.* Third Edition, Columbia University Press, New York, 1963, 1369.

[9] Bender, Great Moments in Medicine, 132-7.

[10] *Ibid.,* 220-6.

[11] Flexner, Simon and Flexner James Thomas, *William Henry Welch and the Heroic Age of American Medicine.* Viking Press, New York, 1941,78.

[12] *Ibid.,* 111-12.

[13] Thomas, Lewis. *The Medussa and the Snail,* Viking, New York, 1979, 163.

[14] *Ibid.,* 169.

[15] Dubos, Rene'. *Man Adapting,* Yale University Press, New Haven, 1965, 28.

[16] Engel, George. *The Need for a New Medical Model: a challenge for biomedicine,* Science, 1977; 196: 129-136.

[17] White, Leslie A. *A Comparative Study of Keresan Medicine Societies,* International Congress of Americanists, Proceedings of 23rd Session, New York, 1930, 604-19. I am grateful to Edie Swan for calling my attention to this work.

[18] Engel, George. The Need for a New Medical Model: a challenge for biomedicine. 129-36.

[19] Hadler, Norton. Regional Backache. *New England Journal of Medicine,* 1986; 325:1090.

[20] Cats-Baril, W and Frymoyer, John. Predictors of low back pain disability. *Clinical Orthopedics,* 1987; 21:89-98.

[21] Boden, S *et al.* Abnormal magnetic-resonance scans of the lumbar spine in asymptomatic subjects. *Journal of Bone and Joint Surgery* 1990;72A:403-08.

[21] Evans, William *et al.* A Cross Sectional Prevalance Study of Lumbar Disc Degeneration in a Working Population, *Spine,* 14:60, 1989.

[21] Powell, M *et al.* Prevalance of Lumbar Disc Degeneration Observed by Magnetic Resonance in Symptomless Women, *Lancet,* 2:1366, 1986.

[21] Wiesel, S *et al.* A Study of Computer-assisted Tomography.I. The Incidence of Positive CAT Scans in an Asymptomatic Group of Patients, *Spine,* 5:324, 1980.

[22] Boden, S. Abnormal Magnetic Resonance Scans of the Lumbar Spine in an Asymptomatic Group of Patients, *J Bone Joint Surg,* 1990, 72A:403-08.

[22] Wiesel, S. The Incidence of Positive CAT Scans in an Asymptomatic Group of Patients. *Spine,* 1984, 9: 549-51.

[23] Jensen, M *et al.* Magnetic Resonance Imaging of the Lumbar Spine in People Without Back Pain, *NEJM,* 331:69-73, 1994.

[24] Thomas, Lewis, *The Medussa and the Snail,* 169.

[25] Battie, M *et al.* A Prospective Study of the Role of Cardiovascular Fitness in Industrial Back Pain Complaints. 141-47.

[25] Bigos, S *et al.* Back Injuries in Industry: a Retrospective Study III Employee Related Factors, 252-56.

[26] Nachemson, Alf. The Solution, Challenge of the Lumbar Spine, San Antonio, Texas, 1988.

[27] Cats-Baril, W and Frymoyer, John. Predictors of Low Back Pain Disability. 89-98.

[27] Naschemson, Alf. Newest Knowledge of Low Back Pain. *Clincial Orthopedic Related Research,* 279:8, 1992.

[28] Rickard, K. The Occurance of Maladaptive Behaviors and Teacher-related Conduct Problems in Children of Chronic Low Back Pain Patients, *Journal of Behavioral Medicine,* 11:107, 1988.

[29] Evans, William. Education: The Primary Treatment of Low Back Pain, Chapter in *Spine Care,* ed White A H and Schofferman J, Mosby, St. Louis, 1995, 347-358.

[30] Waddell, Gordon. A New Clinical Model for the Treatment of Low Back Pain. *Spine,* 1987;12:632-44.

[31] Mulley, A G. Foundation for Informed Decison Making, Patient Back Decison Programs.

[32] Evans, William. Education: The Primary Treatment of Low-Back Pain, 347-358.

[33] White, Lynn, Back School. *State of the Art Reviews,* 1991, Hanley and Belfus.

[34] Knowles, John. Doing Better and Feeling Worse: Health in the United States. W. W. Norton, New York, 1977.

[35] Ingram, Bill. *Medical Tribune Obstetrician and Gynecologist* Edit, 3:18,1986

[36] Hoffman, Catherine. Persons with Chronic Conditions, *JAMA,* 1996, 276:18, 1473-9.

[37] Statement by Roscoe Van Zandt, M.D., August 2, 1995 in a Recommendation for the effectiveness of the Page Bailey Institute.

[38] Page Bailey Teaching Glenwood Springs, Valley View Hospital, March 19, 1997.

[39] Rocky Mountain HMO Post Educotherapy Improvement Assessment Data, Grand Junction Colorado, 1995.

[40] Institute of Medicine. *Medical education and societal needs: a planning report for health professions.* National Academy Press, Washington, D. C., 1983, 93.

[41] Salk, Jonas. *Can Illness Be Prevented,* Limits to Medicine Congress, Gottlieb Dittweiler Institute, Rublikon Zurich, Switzerland, 1975.

[42] Ottawa Charter for Health Promotion, World Health Organization, November 17-21, 1986.

[43] Dubos, René. *Man Adapting,* Yale University Press, New Haven, 1963.

[44] Kass, Leon. *Toward a More Natural Science,* The Free Press, New York, 1985,183.

[45] Center for Disease Control. *Ten Leading Causes of Death in the United States,* 1977, U. S. Government Printing Office, Washinton D. C.

[46] *Ibid.*

[47] Institute of Medicine, *Medical education and societal needs: A Planning report for health professionals.* National Academy Press, Washington, D.C., 1983

[48] Tresolini, Carol. *Health Professions Education and Relationship Centered Care,* 13-67.

[49] This perspective is encompassed in the Health Resilience Paradigm which has been advocated to the Fetzer Foundation, the Pew Health Professions Commision and the National Institutes of Health. For information regarding the Health Resilience Paradigm see resources section at the back of the book.

[50] Oxford English Dictionary. 1961 reprint of 1933 edition, 570-71.

[51] Pell S, Fayerweather W. Trends in the Incidence of Myocardial Infarction and in Associated Mortality and Morbidity in a Large Employed Population 1957-1983. *New Eng J Med,* 1985; 312: 1005-1011.

Kannel W, Dawber T, McGee D. Perspectives on Systolic Hypertension. The Framingham Study. *Circulation* 1980; 61:1179-1182.

Gordon T, Castelli W, Hjortland M, et al. Diabetes, blood lipids, and the role of Obesity in Coronary Heart Disease. The Framingham Study. *Ann Int Med* 1977; 87:393-397.

[52] Fletcher G, Blair S, Blumenthal J, et al. AHA Medical Scientific Statement on Exercise. *Circulation,* 1992; 86:340-4.

Paffenbarger R, Hyde R, Wing A, Hsieh C. Physical Activity, All Cause Mortality, and Longevity of College Alumni. *New Eng J Med,* 1979;314: 605-13.

White P, Mondeika T. Diet and Exercise: Synergism in Health Maintainence, *AMA,* Chicago 1982.

[53] Mendelson J, Mello N. Biologic Concomitants of Alcoholism. *New Eng J Med,* 1979:301:912.

Kissin B, Begleiter H,(eds) *The Biology of Alcoholism.* Plenum, New York, 1975.

[54] Jaffe J. *Drug Addiction and Drug Abuse in The Pharmacologic*

Basis of Therapeutics, 8th Ed A. G. Gilman *et al* (eds).
Mac Millan, New York, 1990; 522-73.

[55] Sinetar, Marsha. *To build the life you want, create the work you love,* St. Martin's Griffin, New York, 1996, 2-193.

[56] Greenfield S, Kaplan S H, Ware J E, Expanding Patient Involvement in Care: Effects on Patient Outcomes. *Ann of Int Med,* 1985; '104(4):520-528.

Greenfield S, Kaplan S H, Ware J E, *et al.* Patient Participation in Medical Care: effects on blood sugar control and quality of life in diabetes. *J Gen Int Med,* Sept-Oct 1988; 448-457.

Greenfield S, Kaplan S H, Ware J E, *et al.* Expanding patient involvement in care: Effects on blood pressure control. Proceeding of National Conference on High Blood Pressure Control, April 1985.

[57] Miller, L and Goldstein, J. More efficient care of diabetic patients in a county hospital setting. *New England Journal of Medicine,* 286:1388, 1972.

[58] Holman H, Magonson P, Long K. Health education for self management has significant and sustained benefits in chronic arthritis. *Trans Assoc Am Phys.* 1989;102(204):204-208.

[59] *Healthy People 2000,* U S Department of Health and Human Services, Washinton D. C., Office of the Asst Sec for Health; 1991 DHHS Publication (PHS) 91-50213.

[60] Showstack J, Fein O, *et al.* Health of the Public. *JAMA,* 1992; 297: 2497-2502.

[61] Schmidt H, Dauphine W, Patel V. Comparing the effects of problem based and conventional curricla in an international sample. *J Med Educ,* 1987; 62:305-315.

Kaufman A, Mennin S, Waterman R, *et al.* The New Mexico Experiment: educational innovation and institutional change. *Acad Med,* 1989; 64:285-294.

Mennin S P, Martinez-Burrola N. The cost of problem-based vs. traditional medical education. *Med Educ,* 1988; 20:187-194.

Moore-West M, Harrington D L, Mennin S P et al, Distress and attitudes toward the learning environment: effects of a curriculum innovation in research in medical education. Proceeding of the annual conference on research on medical education. 1986; 25:292-300.

Moore-West M, O'Donnell M J. Program Evaluation. In Implementing problem-based medical education: lessons from successful innovations. A Kaufman (ed), Springer Publishing Co, New York, 1985; 180-206.

Neufeld V, Barrows H. The McMaster philosophy: an approach to medical education. *J of Med Educ,* 1974; 49: 1040-50.

[62] Salk, *Survival of the Wisest,* 104.

[63] Moore, Robert. Forward in *Ritual,* 9.

[64] Arrien, Angeles. *The Four-Fold Way,* Harper San Francisco, 1993, 49.

[65] *Ibid.,* 49.

[66] *Ibid.,* 50.

[67] *Ibid.,* 50.

[68] Achterberg, Jeanne. *Woman as Healer,* Shambhala, Boston, 1990.

[69] Arrien, Angeles. *Four-Fold Way,* 53

[70] Jonas, S. *A perspective for educating physicians for prevention,* Public Health Reports, 1982; 97:199-204.

[71] Schroeder S, Zone J, Showstack J. Academic Medicine and a Public Trust. *JAMA,* 1989; 262:803-9

[72] 1991-92 *Directory of American Medical Education,* AMA, Chicago.

[73] Bly, Robert. *The Sibling Society,* 57

[74] *Ibid.,* 58-60.

[75] Abram , David. *The Spell of the Sensuous, Perception and Language in a More than Human World,* Pantheon, New York, 1996, 178.

[76] *Ibid.,* 77.

[77] Brennan T, Leape L, Laird N, *et al.* Incidence of adverse events and negligence in hospitalized patients - results of the Harvard Medical Practice Study I, *NEJM,* 1991;324:370-6.

[77] Steel K, Gertman P, Crescenzi C, Anderson J. Iatrogenic illness on a general medical service at a university hospital. *N Eng J Med,* 1981; 304:638-42.

[78] Medical Education and Societal Needs: A planning report for health professions. Institute of Medicine. National Academy Press, Washington D. C. 1983.

[79] Lundberg G. National health care reform: the aura of inevitability intensifies. *JAMA* 1992;267:2521-24.

[80] Auden W, Kronenberger L. *Aphorisms.* Viking, New York, 1966;215.

[81] Osler W. *Counsels and Ideals,* Classics of Medicine Library, Birmingham. 1985:191.

[82] Young Q. *Practical Problems of Drug Abuse.* Presentation at the Limits to Medicine Congress, Davos, Switzerland, Gottlieb Duttweiler Institute. Zurich, 1975.

[83] Avorn J, *et al.* A randomized trial of a program to reduce the use of psychoactive drugs in nursing homes. *N Eng J Med,* 1992;237:168-73.

[84] A paper expressing the concept of Educational Therpuetics within the medical education curriculum has been provided to the New England Journal of Medicine, Journal of the

American Medical Association, the journal Academic
Medicine and major medical schools. The Health Resilience
Paradigm application of the material described in Chapters 4
and 5 has been submitted to the National Institutes of Health
for reduction of low back disability.

[85] Tresolini, *Relationship-Centered Care,* 5-65.

[86] Leonard Duhl of the University of California School of Public
Health Department of Social and Administrative Health
Sciences at Berkeley has written and worked extensively
toward planning and getting a healthy city.

[87] The Page Bailey Institute curriculum for Recovering has been
successful in helping people with a wide variety of chronic
conditions in guiding their nervous systems toward improved
recovery experiences.

[88] Remen, Rachel, "The Recovery of the Sacred-Some thoughts on
medical reform, *In Context,* No. 29, 28.

[89] Evans, William. Education: The Primary Treatment of Low
Back Pain, 353.

[90] This conversation occured prior to a presentation which Dr.
Salk made at the Denver Medical Society Library.

[91] Rennen, Rachel. "The Recovery of the Sacred - Some thoughts
on medical reform." *In Context,* No.29, 28.

[92] Unpublished correlations from the Indian Health Service and
National Hospitalization Data.

[93] Rennen, Rachel. "The Recovery of the Sacred", 29.

[94] U.S. Senator Edward Kennedy, D-Mass quoted by Robert Pear,
*Congress stumbling over itself to regulate HMO's and health
care,* New York Times, March 10, 1997.

[95] Meyerhoff, Barbara. Balancing between Worlds: The Shaman's
Calling, *Parabola,* vol. 1 no.2, 6-13.

[96] I gratefully acknowledge the observations of D. P Sheehan and
David Larson. Many kind and cooperative librarians have
tried to help me localize and acknowledge where their
statements were published, but this has been unsuccessful. I
apologize to those sources. Somewhere in my papers and files
I will locate the missing piece of paper. At the present time I
am still looking on my desk.

[97] Rennen, Rachel. "The Recovery of the Sacred", 30

[98] Abram, David. *The Spell and the Sensuous,* 154-62.

[99] Cameron, Julia, *The Vein of Gold,* 78.

[100] A number of people have made this observation. Jeanne
Achterberg is one who has made the statement.

[101] Saraydarian, Torkom. *Joy and Healing,* 11.

[102] Remen, Rachel, The Recovery of the Sacred, 31

[103] Wilber, Ken. How Big is Our Umbrella, *Noetic Sciences Review,* Winter 1996. No. 40. 10-17.

[104] Palmore, Erdman. Physical, mental and social factors in predicting longevity. *Gerontologist,* 1969, 9: 103-108.

[105] Palmore, Erdman. Predicting longevity: A followup controlling for age. *Gerontologist,* 1969, 9: 247-50.

[106] An ancient teaching of traditional people recorded in *The Walking People* by Paula Underwood, A Tribe of Two Press, San Anselmo, CA

[107] Senge, Peter. *The Fifth Discipline,* 172

[108] Many cultures and teachers have become aware that this passage is necessary to arrive at wisdom. Medical and scientific research are valuable tools to help us penetrate mystery and the unknown. When we are able to hear the rhythm of our heart we may be able to see beyond the limits of investigational research and touch wisdom. Solomon was seen to have wisdom when he was able to choose between two women claiming the same child. See I Kings 3:16-28. In the Greek culture Homer represented the passage through difficult challenges in *The Odyssey,* one route passed between clashing rocks. To avoid sailing that course Odysseus choose instead to steer between Scylla, a sea monster who lived in a cave above the Strait of Mesina, and the whirlpool of Charybdis. Roger Walsh, M.D. calls attention to the lions that guard the gates of Eastern temples. The path to health and wisdom leads beyond where the scientific method and research are able to take us, but it does not ignore the truths discovered by valid studies. None of us want to travel down the road without good medical care. However, despite the great benefits and virtues of what medical research has been able to prove it is unable to guide each of us, as a case of one, the full distance to health, purpose and wisdom. We can learn from Salk the challenge is not *either or,* but rather *and* - to hold respect for both the wisdom of the rhythm of the heart and what research can teach us. I want my children to be able to step into the future with the best medical care possible for my family and me. I also want us to step into the future with all of our parts and our 'right to be.' No one knows what science will come to prove and understand in one hundred years. The essence is that part of us which picks up on important information before science researches it. What the essence can share may or may not be within the realm of what science will be able to prove.

COPYRIGHT ACKNOWLEDGEMENT

About the Author

William Evans grew up on the ridges and rivers of the Rocky Mountains. He is a medical doctor and also holds degrees in traditional Chinese medicine. He has been a visionary founding and developing emergency medical systems and spine rehabilitation programs. He is currently interested in the relationship of purpose to health and is active with educational efforts which reduce disability. His private practice over the past twenty years has been devoted to patients with back pain.